DECORATING WITH
AMERICANA

DECORATING WITH
AMERICANA

How to Know It,
Where to Find It,
and
How to Make It
Work for You

Carter Smith

Oxmoor House®

Dedicated to Betsy, Adair, Carter, and Adam

Copyright © 1985 by Oxmoor House, Inc.
Book Division of Southern Progress Corporation
P.O. Box 2463 Birmingham, Alabama 35201

Library of Congress Catalog Number: 84-60288
ISBN: 0-8487-0627-7

Manufactured in the United States of America
First Printing
Created by Media Projects Incorporated

On the half-title page: "Miss Liberty," a copper weather vane with original polychrome paint. Made by J. Fisk, New York, nineteenth century.
On the title page: This living room in a restored log cabin on Lookout Mountain, Tennessee, is highly sophisticated in its mix of nineteenth-century Pennsylvania furniture, contemporary upholstered pieces, and a "Faithipur" dhurrie rug. *Opposite*: An American chest faithfully reproduced from an eighteenth-century Chippendale piece is pictured here in the foyer of Craft House in Williamsburg.

Table of Contents

Introduction 8
by Carter Smith

How to Create Your Own American Style 18
by Alexandra Stoddard

The Colonial Styles 28

The Federal Styles 58

The American Empire Style   90

The Victorian Styles   114

The Turn-of-the-Century Styles   146

The Eclectic Twentieth-Century Styles   178

Resource Guide   208

Selected Bibliography   218

Acknowledgements   220

Index   221

Opposite: An early-nineteenth-century child's chest is used as a living room side table in a Highlands, North Carolina, home. *Below*: From Maine, an early-twentieth-century hooked rug.

Introduction

Above: Like the rest of the rooms and areas in this Highlands, North Carolina, house (see pages 178–183), the hallway exhibits the owners' tasteful melding of nineteenth-century antiques with contemporary furnishings and crafts. The owners' monogram is worked into the Pennsylvania-style stencil design. *Opposite*: In a cozy weekend house, a wood stove is ready to warm diners seated around a turn-of-the-century "Grand Rapids-style" lion-footed pedestal table. The chairs and table are oak.

The goals of *Decorating with Americana*, as the book's subtitle suggests, are to help readers learn how to identify and locate Americana and how to creatively integrate the great American styles into their living and work spaces.

"Americana," for many of us, means early-American antiques (the U.S. Customs Service classes an antique as any object over one hundred years old). But, a substantial number of us collect American handmade and mass-produced wares of the last thirty to fifty years. Furthermore, magnificent reproduction furniture and accessories are being manufactured today and must be included in a book on decorating with great American styles. We therefore include in *Americana* the wonderfully broad range of decorative objects that have been made by and for Americans, from the craftsmanship of our earliest colonists up through the eclectic styles of the present century.

In the next few pages, I will give a brief survey of style periods of America's principal architectural and decorative arts. In the section that follows, Alexandra Stoddard, one of the country's leading interior designers, provides an illustrated essay, "How to Create Your Own American Style."

Six chapters, based on style periods, illustrate how Americans in dwellings from the smallest farmhouses to the grandest town houses and plantations did and do make these houses "homes"—with style, resourcefulness, and creativity.

At the conclusion of *Decorating with Americana* the reader will find a Selected Bibliography and Resource Guide for both antique and reproduction materials for each of the American style periods.

America's Design Roots

As celebrated in a major 1980 Smithsonian Institution exhibition and book, America is a "nation of nations."

This nation comprises Native Americans; descendants of the early English, French, Dutch, and Spanish colonists; descendants of the myriad national and ethnic groups that have immigrated to this country in the last three centuries. Indeed, many of us are a mixture of several of these groups.

Quite naturally, then, our design roots—our architectural and decorative-arts traditions—are similarly varied.

In the styleline charts that follow, we have traced the evolution of architectural and interior-design styles from the sixteenth century through our own period. You will see houses, furniture, and furnishings for each period.

Many design sources will be represented: ceramics from Holland, Pennsylvania-German painted furniture, armoires in the French manner, Amish quilts, Shaker furniture, and others.

As suggested by the names applied to the early style periods, however—William and Mary, Queen Anne, and Chippendale—the overriding design mode in civilized America in our first three centuries was English.

Styleline 1620–1780

ARCHITECTURE

A seventeenth-century frame house in Farmington, Connecticut.

A Cape Cod cottage.

FURNITURE

A New England turned armchair.

An antique William and Mary style highboy.

TEXTILES, FLOOR & WALL COVERINGS

A reproduction English cotton print in the "Sun, Moon and Stars" pattern [R.G. #233].

LIGHTING & HARDWARE

A museum reproduction of an English seventeenth-century brass candlestick [R.G. #229].

An iron and brass candlestand.

TABLEWARE

Museum reproduction salt and pepper shakers [R.G. #229] after Newport, Rhode Island, originals.

Museum reproduction Wedgwood dinnerware in the "Potpourri" pattern [R.G. #210].

Gunston Hall, a notable plantation house in the Georgian style.

A Kent, Connecticut, frame house in the style known as "salt box."

A "lowboy" or dressing table and two side chairs in the Queen Ann style.

Three Chippendale style side chairs, made in Charleston, South Carolina.

A reproduction of a French wallpaper in the "Morning Glory" pattern [R.G. #229].

A reproduction of an English chintz in the "Andrew Jackson" pattern [R.G. #108].

A reproduction oak and metal chandelier [R.G. #192].

Handwrought iron cooking utensils and holder from the late eighteenth century.

A reproduction tin wall sconce [R.G. #192].

A museum reproduction Chinese Export dinner plate with the arms of the Society of Cincinnati (a veterans' organization of Washington's officers) [R.G. #230].

A museum reproduction of a silver tea and coffee service made in Boston by Paul Revere [R.G. #210].

Styleline 1781–1890

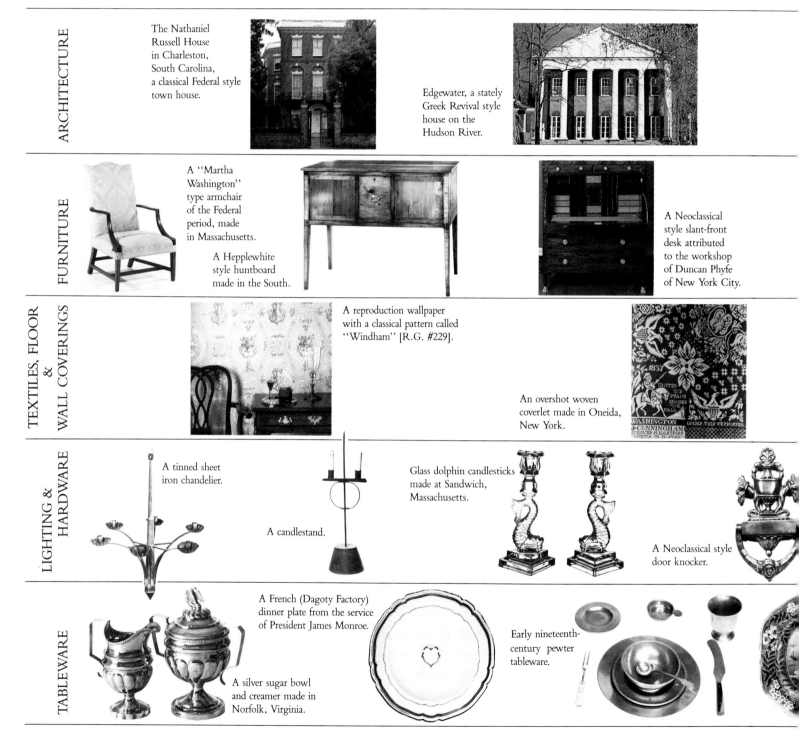

1781   1800   1820

ARCHITECTURE

The Nathaniel Russell House in Charleston, South Carolina, a classical Federal style town house.

Edgewater, a stately Greek Revival style house on the Hudson River.

FURNITURE

A "Martha Washington" type armchair of the Federal period, made in Massachusetts.

A Hepplewhite style huntboard made in the South.

A Neoclassical style slant-front desk attributed to the workshop of Duncan Phyfe of New York City.

TEXTILES, FLOOR & WALL COVERINGS

A reproduction wallpaper with a classical pattern called "Windham" [R.G. #229].

An overshot woven coverlet made in Oneida, New York.

LIGHTING & HARDWARE

A tinned sheet iron chandelier.

A candlestand.

Glass dolphin candlesticks made at Sandwich, Massachusetts.

A Neoclassical style door knocker.

TABLEWARE

A French (Dagoty Factory) dinner plate from the service of President James Monroe.

A silver sugar bowl and creamer made in Norfolk, Virginia.

Early nineteenth-century pewter tableware.

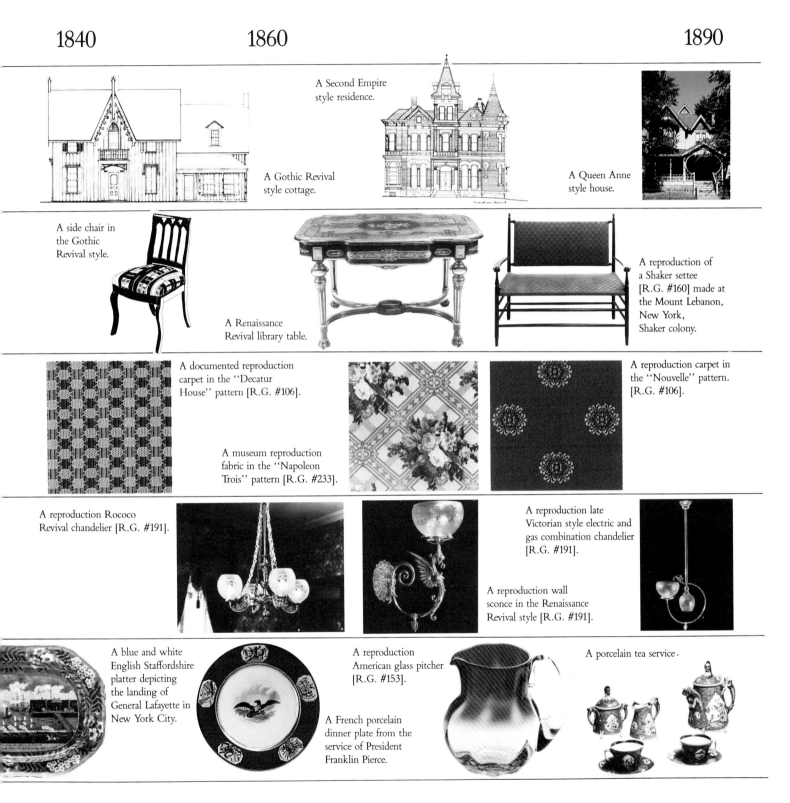

1840   1860   1890

A Second Empire style residence.

A Gothic Revival style cottage.

A Queen Anne style house.

A side chair in the Gothic Revival style.

A Renaissance Revival library table.

A reproduction of a Shaker settee [R.G. #160] made at the Mount Lebanon, New York, Shaker colony.

A documented reproduction carpet in the "Decatur House" pattern [R.G. #106].

A reproduction carpet in the "Nouvelle" pattern. [R.G. #106].

A museum reproduction fabric in the "Napoleon Trois" pattern [R.G. #233].

A reproduction Rococo Revival chandelier [R.G. #191].

A reproduction late Victorian style electric and gas combination chandelier [R.G. #191].

A reproduction wall sconce in the Renaissance Revival style [R.G. #191].

A blue and white English Staffordshire platter depicting the landing of General Lafayette in New York City.

A reproduction American glass pitcher [R.G. #153].

A porcelain tea service.

A French porcelain dinner plate from the service of President Franklin Pierce.

13

Styleline 1891–1983

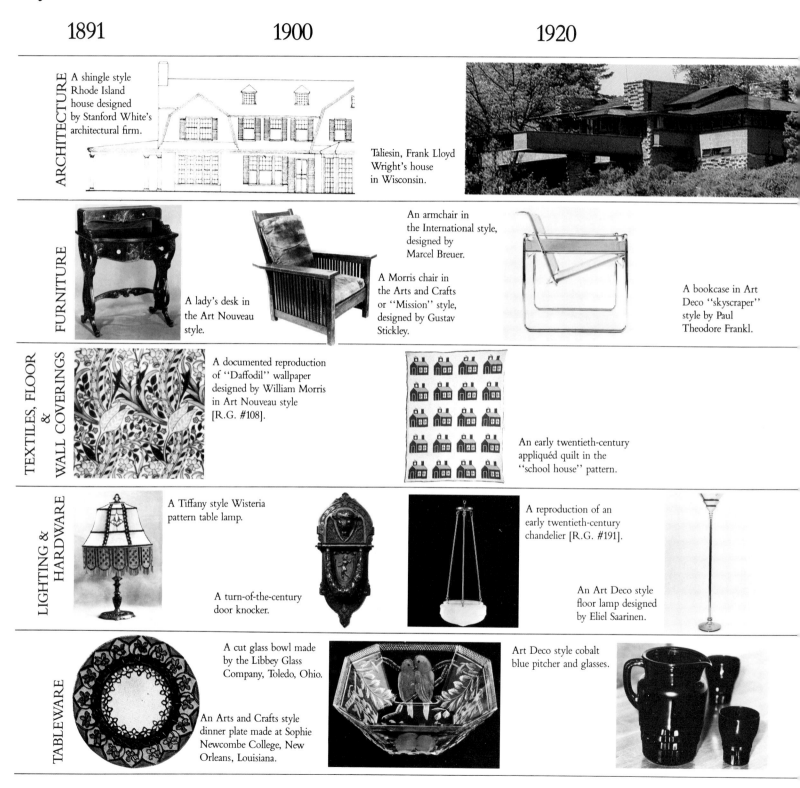

1891

1900

1920

ARCHITECTURE

A shingle style Rhode Island house designed by Stanford White's architectural firm.

Taliesin, Frank Lloyd Wright's house in Wisconsin.

FURNITURE

A lady's desk in the Art Nouveau style.

A Morris chair in the Arts and Crafts or "Mission" style, designed by Gustav Stickley.

An armchair in the International style, designed by Marcel Breuer.

A bookcase in Art Deco "skyscraper" style by Paul Theodore Frankl.

TEXTILES, FLOOR & WALL COVERINGS

A documented reproduction of "Daffodil" wallpaper designed by William Morris in Art Nouveau style [R.G. #108].

An early twentieth-century appliquéd quilt in the "school house" pattern.

LIGHTING & HARDWARE

A Tiffany style Wisteria pattern table lamp.

A turn-of-the-century door knocker.

A reproduction of an early twentieth-century chandelier [R.G. #191].

An Art Deco style floor lamp designed by Eliel Saarinen.

TABLEWARE

A cut glass bowl made by the Libbey Glass Company, Toledo, Ohio.

An Arts and Crafts style dinner plate made at Sophie Newcombe College, New Orleans, Louisiana.

Art Deco style cobalt blue pitcher and glasses.

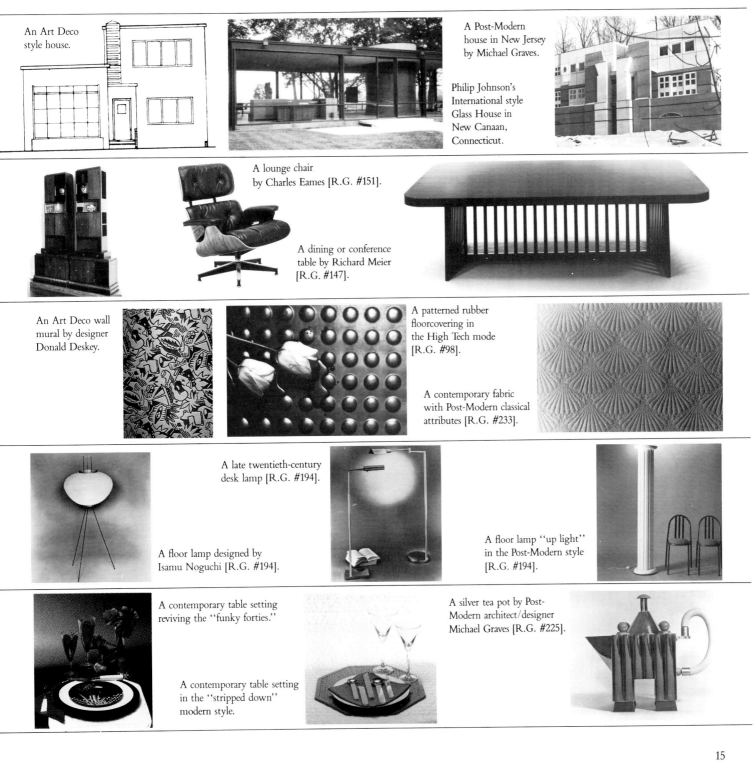

An Art Deco style house.

A Post-Modern house in New Jersey by Michael Graves.

Philip Johnson's International style Glass House in New Canaan, Connecticut.

A lounge chair by Charles Eames [R.G. #151].

A dining or conference table by Richard Meier [R.G. #147].

An Art Deco wall mural by designer Donald Deskey.

A patterned rubber floorcovering in the High Tech mode [R.G. #98].

A contemporary fabric with Post-Modern classical attributes [R.G. #233].

A late twentieth-century desk lamp [R.G. #194].

A floor lamp designed by Isamu Noguchi [R.G. #194].

A floor lamp "up light" in the Post-Modern style [R.G. #194].

A contemporary table setting reviving the "funky forties."

A contemporary table setting in the "stripped down" modern style.

A silver tea pot by Post-Modern architect/designer Michael Graves [R.G. #225].

15

Robert Frost wrote:

The land was ours before we were the land's.
...she was ours
In Massachusetts, In Virginia
But we were England's, still
colonials...

By the year 1700, British colonists had settled along the Atlantic seacoast from Massachusetts to South Carolina. As they cleared the wilderness, they created "little Englands," both in the architecture of their typically simple homes and in their furnishings. To a lesser degree the same was to happen in the Spanish style in the Southwest and in the French manner along the Mississippi and the Gulf Coast. (On the East Coast, exceptions to the English influence were found in Dutch settlements in New York and German settlements in Pennsylvania.)

When and how, then, did a uniquely American style emerge?

In his authoritative *American Furniture and the British Tradition to 1830*, John Kirk writes, "American furniture paralleled European, especially British, models until the late nineteenth century, when styles became less dependent on a particular center, and more international in scope."

Kirk also points out that American furniture makers tended to emulate British rural craftsmen rather than those in such "high-style centers" as London or Dublin.

Early American-made furniture, then, was somewhat derivative and perhaps unsophisticated. (A notable eighteenth-century exception was to be found at Newport, Rhode Island, where a "school" of gifted cabinetmakers created a number of distinctively American pieces.)

Of course, American furniture makers used native materials, including the wide boards taken from the virgin forests of walnut, maple, and cherry.

Just as American architecture reflected the needs of each region—wide porches in the South, steeply pitched roofs to avoid snow buildup in the North—so did the furniture. In the Northeast, for example, the high-backed settle was a popular form. Typically, it would be placed close to the fireplace, with its back to the front door, to retain the cherished warmth of the fire. In the South, a favorite piece of furniture was the huntboard, a high sideboard at which hunters home from the fields would stand and have a drink or two.

Readers will find more and more rooms and pieces with a distinctly American look as they proceed chronologically through our style periods. Native American saddle blankets, beautifully carved decoys, colorful quilts and hooked rugs, all have this indefinable but unmistakable look.

In fact, a friend reports with great pride that in a Paris subway a French matron pointed at her woven hand basket, smiled, and said, "Ah, Nantucket, oui?" Right!

But the American look goes far beyond the objects themselves. Our hallmark, as Alexandra Stoddard writes, is in the creative mixing of styles from our rich and diverse cultural heritage.

Carter Smith

Above left: This room in a lovingly restored hacienda in New Mexico reflects the simple, strongly spiritual life-style of our Hispanic forebears in the Southwest. The rug is Navajo; the tin candelabrum and crucifix are probably Mexican. *Left*: The English taste has prevailed in America not only because the English were by the eighteenth century by far the largest colonial ethnic group, but also because the leading English cabinetmakers published stylebooks, a valuable resource for American craftsmen. The American maker of this elegant chair may well have followed Thomas Chippendale's *Gentleman and Cabinet Maker's Director*, which enhanced the popularity of the Chippendale style in this country as well as in England. *Above middle*: This little cypress table, with graceful cabrioles in the Louis XVI style, was made in Louisiana by a French emigré in the late eighteenth century. *Above*: This room in the Winterthur Museum is from a 1755 house in Berks County, Pennsylvania. Crafted in the style of the county's German settlers, the furnishings include a "sawbuck" table (1750–1800), walnut "plank" chairs (1770–1830), a richly painted blanket chest, armchairs, and a large scrank (wardrobe).

17

How to Create Your Own American Style

Above: Eighteenth-century Chippendale furniture, nineteenth-century
silver candlesticks, contemporary mirror mats, glass and fresh flowers are
mixed in a classically beautiful table setting. *Right*: The owners' wit
and color sense are clear in this Lookout Mountain, Tennessee, kitchen.
Animal images in early twentieth-century advertising are integrated
with folk carvings and flowering houseplants. The pine serving table is
Southern; the chair is from an ice cream parlor.

In America in the turbulent 1980s we can use all the good news we can get, and the emerging interior design trends are just that: a blessed return to light, beauty, a respect for things traditionally American, and, above all, personal style. Happily behind us is the vogue for high-tech furnishing and the Spartan "less is more" look.

Still very much with us is the love for things of our heritage. The "country look," which integrated folk art, crafts, and even primitive country antiques into our design schemes, has been augmented by a somewhat more formal and eclectic design approach.

As you have read in Carter Smith's Introduction, from the earliest Colonial times we have been a nation of individualists in the way we dressed our homes. Never purists, we mixed European wares brought to America from the old country with furniture and accessories made here. Some were made by master craftsmen

Above: The designer Alexandra Stoddard created an informal mood in the sitting area of her master bedroom by bleaching the floor and combining nineteenth-century wicker with an eighteenth-century pine chest, thumb-back chair, and milking stool. American nineteenth-century appliqué quilts and a handmade mohair throw add charm, color, and warmth. A painting by Roger Muhl hangs over the loveseat. The pastel fabric that covers the furniture is called "Joy"; the inspiration for the pattern was a monk's garden seen by Miss Stoddard in the south of France.

in style centers such as Boston, New York, Philadelphia, and Charleston; other furnishings were created in country workshops.

Further, today's arbiters of taste—the interior designers and the home-furnishing industry—seem to agree that most people more than ever want their homes to make a strong personal statement and not have the "done" look characterized by such recent styles as high-tech, international, and English country.

How, then, to decide on your own interior-design goals and choose the style that is right for you?

For me, and many of the clients I assist, any decorating project begins with basic homework, followed by some outside research.

My advice is to start with an inspiration file. One client of mine uses a pretty pastel box left over from a nightgown purchase at a department store; another uses colorful folders. You might want to start a scrapbook. Gather pictures out of magazines, gallery brochures, auction catalogs, even seed catalogs. Add to your collection scraps of things you admire: a delicious color you found inside the lining of an envelope perhaps, or the giftwrapping paper and ribbon that came with a package you liked. Hold on to snips of fabric, trims, and gimps that appeal to you.

Devise a system for labeling each of the items you collect. Write down what details you are attracted to or use arrows. Be specific. If you clip out a room interior from a magazine, analyze what you especially admire. As you go along, you may want to create individual folders for different living spaces—living rooms, bedrooms, kitchens.

As your file expands, think of it as a collage—an adventure in artistic composition of colors, materials, and forms. You will discover that the unifying components come from the breadth and depth of your life experience. Nothing you envision will be absolutely new, but your interpretation of what you see will make each design uniquely your own.

Next, open your closet; look at the colors, textures, and patterns of your wardrobe. Do the same for the rest of your family. We are all most comfortable and happiest in rooms—as in clothes —that we feel are most flattering.

Out of these colors and patterns and clippings, a sense of your individual taste and flair will emerge.

It is now time to apply your taste to the decorating projects on your agenda. A good beginning is to make an inventory of everything you own. Give everything a lot number, just as auction houses do, and photograph the important pieces. You may want to have your silver and furniture appraised by a registered appraiser or an auction gallery. Some will do this without charge, from a photograph or from examination of the object. (The inventory is important for insurance purposes as well.)

Once you have an inventory and know the dollar value (as well as the sentimental value) of what you own, make a priority list. If you are a saver, a conservationist, a preservationist, or just a sentimental pack rat, you will have to go through your list several times and do some soul-searching if you need to part with things.

Trust your instinct. If you love something, you will want to be its keeper. Put these items at the top of your priority list.

Now, as to decorating with Americana: Most of our inventories and favorite clippings will include a number of antiques or recent classic pieces made by American craftsmen or manufacturers. Because Americana is one of the categories of antiques that are

Above: Reflections in the mirrored wall of a long, narrow entrance hall: Antique duck decoys appear to float on a bleached and stained, stenciled chevron-design floor. A basket of dried field flowers and herbs rests like a miniature island among the ducks.

Above: This bedroom rug was designed and hooked by George Wells, who incorporated in the design all the favorite animals of his childhood on his grandmother's ranch. The family place has a series of red barns and, like the rug, is bordered by a picket fence.

rapidly rising in value, it is unlikely that you will consign these pieces in your inventory to the attic, the auction house, or the thrift shop of your favorite charity.

How then to create a personal American style in your home?

With this volume, with the books listed in the Selected Bibliography, and from visits to museum houses, you can categorize and hone your own favorite American pieces by style period and by their function relative to the rooms in your house.

You will see, in the interior views of the museum houses and private homes that follow, that *it is not necessary to decorate a house, or room, of a certain architectural period solely with furnishings of that period.* Eighteenth-century houses were filled with American-, English-, and even French-made furniture from all the style periods: Pilgrim Century, William and Mary, Queen Anne, Chippendale, and Federal. Similarly, in the nineteenth century, city and country homes contained heirloom furnishings from earlier times, and as the century progressed, they accumulated the new styles: American Empire, Mid-Victorian Revival, and late nineteenth century. Finally, as you will see in the last two chapters, there has been a diverse and eclectic mixing of styles in twentieth-century interiors.

Some styles will appeal to you more than others, and your possessions, classic and otherwise, will fit better with some styles than with others. For example, although Colonial and Federal high-style furniture seem to meld nicely, they don't mix too well with some of the cruder, but no less attractive, "country" pieces. Similarly, the florid Victorian styles don't harmonize with simple nineteenth-century Shaker.

Whatever the scope of your decorating project, and whether you will be your own decorator or will hire a professional interior designer, you will need a budget, be it $1,000, $10,000, or $100,000.

When you establish your budget, be sure you have a contingency amount of no less than 15 percent above your basic figure. There are always things we forget and last-minute add-ons. And don't overlook maintenance: windows have to be washed, floors waxed or resanded, paint may need touching up. Also, trucking and deliveries can run over budget, and then there's the sales tax.

Before you allot money to specifics, you should analyze your space from an architectural/functional point of view. How is the room to be used? Which of the rooms will be needed for more than one function? There are rooms for different hours and occupations. How many people will use the room? What kind of storage is required? Is present lighting (natural and man-made) appropriate? How formal or informal should the room feel?

Basic architectural flaws must be faced and fixed. If the ceiling is too low, how can it be treated? If the windows aren't right, can they be altered?

Once your rooms are evaluated, make a master plan for your entire space.

First, *don't accept the names as they are labeled.* Maybe two small rooms can become one dramatic space. For example, in a delightful Charleston town house, we removed a pantry between a kitchen and sitting room; and, with those dividing walls gone, we had four light exposures and a charming, sunny kitchen/family room.

Having considered and budgeted these structural concerns, you should next break up each room into these elements:

> *floors*
> *walls and ceilings*
> *color*
> *lighting*
> *windows*
> *fabrics*
> *furniture*
> *accessories*
> *maintenance*

Review the possibilities for each element in each room. For example, a floor accounts for about one-third of a room. In some cases carpeting or area rugs are the answer. *(See the Resource Guide for documented period rugs, carpeting, and floor cloths.)* Wood, however, is in many cases ideal. With wood you can bleach or stencil, spatter or stain. And the grains of American hardwood floors blend beautifully with our wooden furniture of all periods.

The ceiling and the walls of each room are also basics. Happily, the interest in historic restoration and period decorating has made it possible for the paint, wall covering, and fabric industries to manufacture a vast range of colors and patterns in each of the American style periods.

Archaeologists have uncovered the original paint colors in Williamsburg, Savannah, and elsewhere, and manufacturers have matched them faithfully. These documented colors are available from several paint companies that are listed in this volume's Resource Guide.

Such documentation has also been done for a broad range of wallpapers and fabrics. Many of these were imported English and French papers and fabrics but are now being reproduced by American manufacturers.

Above: Red-marble counters four inches thick, butter-cream lacquered walls, and wooden stools painted with images of pigs and cows set the tone in this all-American Texas kitchen. "Vegetable Garden," a large hand-hooked rug by George Wells, graces the wall between the window shutters. The fresh watermelon is from the garden.

Above: The sense of history in this attractive nineteenth-century Nantucket house is evoked by the early-American primitive portrait that hangs over a tea table accented with a generous bouquet of fresh flowers from the garden.

Opposite: Traditional hand-painted pottery plates, cups, and saucers from Brittany add charm to an otherwise typical American dining room. A corner cupboard houses a collection of spatterware and majolica; a candleholder and hanging plate rack decorate the walls. The brass chandelier is Williamsburg in design, and the hand-painted vine stencil border under the cornice molding adds another American touch.

Above: Details highlight the entrance hall of this large and gracious nineteenth-century Charleston house. The documentary stencil wallpaper, a butter-yellow background with a white fan-shaped motif, is "Exeter," by Brunschwig & Fils. A lacy gallery window illuminates a Victorian two-tier table. The old box lock on the front door was probably made by a local ironsmith.

Above: This family room was created by removing the pantry off the dining room and opening the sitting area into the kitchen. Shiny white walls of Swedish emolj paint contrast with the real cork floor. The green leather-covered "planter's chair" has been passed down through the family.

Opposite page: A lively Amish quilt covers a sofa that sits before a lovely Palladian window. Huge ficus trees bring the outdoors in.

After you have arrived at, and budgeted for, the basic background colors and textures for a room, and made decisions about the fabric treatments for windows and upholstered furniture, it will be time to create a "want list" for furniture and accessories that will fit harmoniously and functionally into each space.

Having done your homework—in this and other books, magazines, and museum homes—you are ready to deal with two fundamental questions:

1. How strictly do you want to conform to a particular style? (Some of my friends are mad for Queen Anne. One collects only Southern furniture, except upholstered pieces. As in most homes illustrated in this book, most of us—for reasons of both taste and money—mix styles judiciously.)

2. Must all your American furniture and accessories (such as lighting fixtures, ceramic wares) be original, or will you be happy with some reproductions? (Unless you're John Rockefeller, who founded Williamsburg, or Henry du Pont, who gave us Winterthur, you will likely be happy with some of the beautifully and authentically reproduced furniture and furnishings being manufactured today, many in conjunction with the historic museums' collections.)

In any case, our Resource Guide lists respected manufacturers of reproductions, dealers specializing in American antiques, and regional auction houses (for those who, like me, love an opportunity to bargain hunt).

A final word about decorating your home: even beyond your color schemes and creative mix of furniture, fabrics, and fixtures, you will make each space your own by the paintings and graphics you hang, the collections you display, and those fresh flowers you arrange so deftly.

Master plan, want list, and checkbook ready? Good luck, good hunting, and *good fun*!

Alexandra Stoddard

The Colonial Styles 1620–1783

The house at *left* is Gunston Hall, the home of George Mason, a friend and Potomac River neighbor of George Washington. Begun before 1755, this Georgian-style plantation house is a masterpiece of architectural detail inside and out. *Above:* A still life of top quality eighteenth- and early nineteenth-century furniture and accessories: a

Connecticut Queen Anne dressing table, ca. 1730; two Rhode Island side chairs, also in the Queen Anne style; brass candlesticks; an eighteenth-century Chinese Export tureen; and two early nineteenth-century portraits by Ammi Phillips.

The Colonial period in American history covers a span of 176 years, from the first settlement in Virginia through America's victory in the War for Independence in 1783.

The first colonists settled at Jamestown in 1607. In 1610 the survivors of those first hard years were saved by the arrival of supplies from England, without which the colony would have failed. But archaeologists have found that even during their struggle to establish homes in the wilderness, these early colonists attempted to furnish their habitations with style.

Mostly, though, the rigors of the struggle for survival in the American colonies left little time for creating homes of architectural distinction, or even of comfort. Early Massachusetts Bay colonists could only "burrow themselves in the earth for their first shelter under some hillside, casting the earth aloft upon timber."

These "poore wigwames" were followed in the colonies by simple log houses, a structural form

Left: The Palladian room, or formal parlor, in Gunston Hall contains examples of the finest details and carvings of the Colonial period. George Mason designed the house and started its construction before 1755, then brought over William Buckland, a master craftsman from England, to complete the details. *Above:* Made in Charleston, South Carolina, in the late eighteenth century, this unusual triple chest is a fine example of a form popular in that city.

described by a Virginia traveler on the Virginia frontier in 1780 as "cabins built of unhewn logs and without windows. Kitchen, dining room, bedroom, and hall are all in one room into which one enters when the door opens. The chimney is built at the gable end, of unhewn logs looking like trees, or it is omitted altogether." At the same time, however, in cities such as Williamsburg, Georgian-style homes, churches, and government buildings were being erected.

During what has been termed the "Pilgrim Century" (1607–1685), few colonists were able to bring furnishings with them on the crowded ships or to afford the expensive imported wares—furniture, ceramics, and fabrics.

31

Above: This classic New England center-hall saltbox has been lovingly restored by its owners and is now listed in the National Register of Historic Places. Although its furnishings are "of the period," this weekend retreat is not treated as a museum: a gambrel-roofed wing containing a modern kitchen, bathrooms, service areas, and children's rooms was built behind the original structure. *Above right*: This New-England-made chair (ca. 1740–1760) combines William and Mary style turned legs and a Queen Anne curved back.

The styles in the English colonies were mirrors of those in England. The medieval style (as exemplified in the room view on page 33) was replaced in the early eighteenth century by the William and Mary style, a more ornate style sometimes utilizing applied veneers and inlay. Walnut was the favored primary wood used for crafting William and Mary furniture, and the veneers were often walnut burl (an irregularly grained growth on a tree).

The next great style period, Queen Anne (after the next British monarch), covered the period 1720–1750. This was a time in which increased migration from England to America was paralleled by increased prosperity. The cruder houses of earlier years were replaced or modified, creating larger dwellings with separate rooms for the various domestic needs. In furniture, the upholstered "easy chair" and the daybed or couch came into prominence *(see page 48)*. The Queen Anne designs represented a radical shift to more delicate proportions with graceful slender cabriole legs. Native cherry was added to the list of popular woods, and mahogany was imported for "high-style" furniture.

The Queen Anne period in the colonies also saw a rise in "regionalism" in design, with craftsmen in New England and the Middle Atlantic and Southern cities creating their own separate style variations.

Above: The parlor in this Kent, Connecticut, house *(exterior shown on facing page)* contains a corner cupboard that was original to the house, a maple sofa from Massachusetts (ca. 1800), a Massachusetts tea table (ca. 1770), a Connecticut desk (ca. 1775), and a Massachusetts armchair (ca. 1780) upholstered in a reproduction of an eighteenth-century wool damask.

This creative urge was to continue throughout the last great Colonial style period, the Chippendale (1750–1785), named for the English cabinetmaker Thomas Chippendale, whose furniture-design book *The Gentleman and Cabinet-Maker's Director* set the style in the old country, and soon after in America. His ornate designs included shells, scrolls, and leaves. Furniture legs were either straight or cabriole and had a variety of carved feet.

In architecture, handsome Georgian-style houses of brick, such as Gunston Hall *(see pages 28–30)*, were created as showpieces by wealthy Southern planters and Eastern merchants.

The development of the other decorative arts in Colonial America—ceramics, needlework, metalwork, glass—evolved in much the same pattern as did furniture making. The early colonists imported ceramics or made do with simple, local, wooden tableware called "treen."

The weaving of both clothing and household fabrics was begun in the earliest settlements, but few seventeenth- or eighteenth-century examples of cushions, chair seats, or bed coverings survive. Only the richest homes had imported rugs.

Silversmiths are known to have been working in Boston as early as 1650, and splendid examples of the work of our most celebrated eighteenth-century silversmith, Paul Revere, are in both museum and reproduction collections *(see pages 55–57).*

The owners of the Kent, Connecticut, saltbox shown on these and the preceding pages are avid collectors. The inventory of possessions left by the original owner is a resource they draw upon heavily in furnishing the house in its authentic early style. The dining room, *opposite page* and *above right*, was originally a bedroom. The major elements include two eighteenth-century chests, Chippendale-style chairs (ca. 1770), a maple-topped gate-leg table, and a tavern table, all from Massachusetts. The chest of drawers, *above*, also Massachusetts-made, dates from before 1750. The English delftware bowl (ca. early eighteenth century), *right,* is similar to those illustrated in the room views.

One of the most interesting rooms in the Kent house is the old kitchen, *above* . The paneling still bears its original red paint. The pine settle is from Massachusetts (ca. 1800); the table, a single piece of pine on a maple and oak frame, was probably made in Connecticut in the late 1600s; the black-painted bannister-back armchair is also of Connecticut origin. *Left:* A similar bannister-back side chair, Connecticut (ca. 1700). *Opposite page*: Another view of the Kent house's old kitchen shows an unusual folding table. The New England side chair (ca. 1750) combines William and Mary with Queen Anne features and is similar to the chair illustrated on page 34.

Above: Log Folly, owned by a New Jersey antiques dealer and his family, is a wonderful example of the success achieved by an enthusiastic collector undaunted by the prospect of moving a house from its original site. Built in the mid-nineteenth century in Emigsville, Pennsylvania, the house is now comfortably perched above a stream in Delaware. In order to accommodate a family and provide the amenities of modern living, the owners constructed a wing (visible at right) in the 1960s using the wonderful paneling and interior woodwork they had salvaged from several Maryland houses. The pent eave visible in the front of the house was erected to make a porch. *Above right:* The library of Log Folly, located in the new wing, contains woodwork from a house in Preston, Maryland. The owners have chosen to use the interior of a magnificent Connecticut desk-and-bookcase to display their collection of eighteenth-century miniature salt-glaze wares. Next to that piece is a built-on cupboard that houses another ceramic collection—Chinese Export polychrome enamels made between the early eighteenth and early nineteenth centuries. *Right:* This elegant mahogany side chair with its pierced splat in the Chippendale style was made in South Carolina in the mid-eighteenth century. It is attributed to Thomas Elfe, a prominent Charleston cabinetmaker.

Below: In this view of the Log Folly library two handsome walnut corner chairs flank a five-legged mahogany gaming table. The slab table against the left wall has a distinguished history of ownership in the Van Rensselaer family of Albany, New York. All of these pieces were made in New York between 1730 and 1760. The sofa in the background is of New England origin, while the one in the foreground was made in Philadelphia in about 1770. To the right is a mid-eighteenth century Newport mahogany Pembroke table. The upholstered side chair is a distinctive combination of two furniture forms—the slipper chair and the back stool. *Left:* Another example of the craft of Thomas Elfe is this mahogany Pembroke table. The delicately carved fretwork of the apron is derived from designs in Thomas Chippendale's *Gentleman and Cabinetmaker's Director.*

Above: Painted furniture enlivens this Log Folly bedroom. The blue bed, one of a pair, is of the type used by children or hired hands in Pennsylvania, where they were made in the late eighteenth century. Colorful nineteenth-century appliquéd quilts are here used as bedspreads. The slant-front desk, armchair with turned spindles, and painted chest of drawers were all made in Massachusetts at the turn of the eighteenth century. The painted blanket chest is of Pennsylvania origin, ca. 1780.
Below right: The mantelpiece in the Log Folly master bedroom was taken from a house in Chestertown, Maryland. On, and flanking, the chimney breast is a set of four hand-colored engravings from a series called *Twelve Months of Flowers.* Published in London in 1730, these engravings have descended in the owner's family. The tall-post bed and bonnet-top chest-on-chest were made in Connecticut, ca. 1770. The exquisite bedspread and valances were hand-embroidered by the owner's wife, using a design based on extant examples of eighteenth-century crewel bedhangings. The New England mahogany easy chair and the Philadelphia walnut armchair both date from the mid-eighteenth century.
Above right: This painted poplar blanket chest, decorated with a tulip motif, was made in the Valley of Virginia in the early nineteenth century.

Above: Original to Log Folly is the floor of sun-dried bricks in what is now a breakfast room adjacent to the kitchen. The bricks bear raccoon and dog footprints impressed before they were dried. The painted Pennsylvania corner cupboard houses a collection of eighteenth- and early-nineteenth-century Pennsylvania redware. The pine hanging cupboard, ca. 1770, is also from Pennsylvania. The maple chest of drawers was made in Massachusetts, ca. 1710. The painting depicts a scene in the Covent Garden Coffee House in the eighteenth century.
Left: Early nineteenth-century paintings of Chinese ports, made for export to the West, hang above one of a pair of Chinese armchairs made during the Ming dynasty (1368–1644). Through the door, in the hallway of Log Folly, a mahogany looking-glass of English or American origin hangs over a marble-topped table with Marlborough legs that was crafted in Massachusetts for John Trumbull, Governor of Connecticut between 1769 and 1783.

The Connecticut farmer's cottage, *left*, now a weekend house for a New York City family, provides an interesting case history in architectural evolution. Research suggests it was initially erected as a one-room house with a chimney on the left. Then a second room was added on the other side of the chimney. Later, in the 1840s, a kitchen was added on the rear (note the attic, or "eyebrow," window typical of the period). Finally, the present owners added a new bedroom wing, or ell, with a salt-box roof in the Colonial style. *Below:* The current parlor—the house's first room —contains furnishings made in many style periods, from Colonial to contemporary. The cherrywood corner cupboard is from Kentucky (ca. 1820); the paintings of family ancestors are Victorian, as is the six-board chest; the sofa, rug, and side chair are contemporary. *Opposite page:* Details of the room. A gate-leg Connecticut table (ca. 1740) with original red paint; a Massachusetts corner chair (ca. 1800); a copper weather vane (ca. 1900).

46

The bedroom *above* is another of the beautifully executed rooms in Gunston Hall. As in the Palladian drawing room shown on page 30, the paneling was designed and carved by two English craftsmen brought over by George Mason on four-year indentures. The tester bed is American Chippendale, probably from Philadelphia. The stool at its foot accommodated storage—or a chamber pot—under its seat. The lolling chair, American (ca. 1790), is a type often called a Martha Washington chair. The portrait above the mantel is of Mason's sister, Mary Mason Selden, attributed to Gustavis Hessalius, a leading eighteenth-century American portraitist. *Above left:* A late-eighteenth-century bed rug crafted of wool hooked through a loosely woven linen. *Left:* An eighteenth-century Connecticut cherrywood dressing table, a form sometimes called a lowboy. *Opposite:* An eighteenth-century American cherrywood chest-on-chest.

The owners of this Richmond, Virginia, house have since the 1950s sought examples of early American furniture, concentrating on pieces made in the South. Their collection of examples made before 1830 is installed in a house built in this century, its design based on a Tidewater, Virginia, merchant's house. All of the floors, woodwork, and hardware were removed from late-eighteenth- and early-nineteenth-century Virginia houses. *Above:* In the front hall, along the right-hand wall, is a solid walnut gate-leg table made ca. 1720 and found in Louisa County, Virginia. Above it hangs a likeness of a New England clergyman by an unknown artist. The bannister-back chair with a distinctive crest rail and original red paint is one of a pair, and was probably made in New England, ca. 1740. Against the rear wall is a southwestern Virginia or northeastern North Carolina stretcher-base table, ca. 1720. The thickness of the wood planks used for the skirt and stretcher indicates a rural origin. *Above right:* Typical of furniture made in Tidewater, Virginia, is the impressive mid-eighteenth-century desk-and-bookcase in the library of the Richmond house. Drawn up to it is a Pennsylvania bow-back Windsor armchair, ca. 1750. On top of the desk is a polychrome figure of a militiaman, probably carved in the Valley of Virginia in the early nineteenth century. Above the handsome William-and-Mary-style daybed is a hanging cupboard made in Virginia in the mid-eighteenth century. The Pennsylvania slat-back armchair

partially visible in the foreground dates from the early eighteenth century. *Below:* This pine settle was made in America in the early nineteenth century. Furniture for dual purposes came into use about this time. This piece was designed to function as either a chair or a table.

Above right: The English oak dresser in the breakfast room of the Richmond house, next to the kitchen, accommodates a collection of American and English pewter. The oak gate-leg table has a history of ownership in Virginia and was found between Culpeper and Fredericksburg. The pair of ladder-back chairs was made in the Delaware valley between 1720 and 1750. Also from Delaware is the bow-back Windsor armchair, which dates from about 1790 and is branded by its maker, Sampson Barnet. The Pennsylvania settle, ca. 1800, has its original red paint. The oil painting, dated 1887, is a copy of *A Pastoral Visit—The Minister Comes to Dinner,* painted by Richard Norris Brooke in 1886. *Above left, left,* and *below:* Other fine examples of a ladder-back chair, Windsor chairs, and a Virginia daybed.

Above: The owners of this East Coast collection have, since their marriage in the 1940s, focused their attention on fine examples of eighteenth-century American furniture. Recently, however, they have become attracted to American folk art and have successfully incorporated fine examples into the decor of their home. The living room contains high-style examples of early American furniture, such as the mahogany desk-and-bookcase made in Newport between 1760 and 1780. Displayed in the shelves is a collection of eighteenth-century English and American glassware. Drawn up to the desk-and-bookcase is an eighteenth-century New England mahogany armchair. The wall sconces are English, ca. 1750. The pair of Rhode Island mahogany side chairs to the right of the desk-and-bookcase, ca. 1760, stand on either side of a Philadelphia mahogany pedestal table. The New England easy chair of 1740–1750 flanks an eighteenth-century Philadelphia mahogany candlestand. The small mahogany slant-front desk, part of a large collection of child's furniture and cabinetmaker's samples, was made in New England during the eighteenth century. *Right:* This cherry tea table with scalloped apron, cabrioles, and pad feet was made in Connecticut in the early eighteenth century. It displays the delicate proportions and graceful lines that are hallmarks of the Queen Anne style. *Above right:* This upholstered walnut easy chair with turned stretchers and cabrioles has a fluid arched crest rail. It was made in Massachusetts in the early eighteenth century.

Above: In the bar room, the owners have installed several pieces of American folk art with its natural complement—country furniture. Hanging over the fireplace is a copper trotter weather vane made in the nineteenth century. The maple tavern table, ca. 1740, retains its original dark-red paint. The Windsor armchair to the right was made in Rhode Island, ca. 1780–1800. The New England walnut table in the foreground dates from about 1750. Next to the table is a child's Windsor chair of the early nineteenth century. The cigar-store Indian was carved in the late nineteenth century. Of New England origin are another child's Windsor chair and the upholstered armchair, both mid-eighteenth century. *Above left:* This eighteenth-century mahogany pole screen, a rare survival, retains its original flame-stitch needlework panel. It was made between 1740 and 1760, and has descended in several Boston families. *Left:* Another example of a child's Windsor chair, ca. 1750.

Overleaf: In the entrance hall of the East Coast home an English seventeenth-century brass candlestick and an American glass bottle grace an eighteenth-century New England candlestand. The portraits, of Mr. and Mrs. Jacob Einzig of Lancaster County, Pennsylvania, were painted by Jacob Eichholtz, a prolific portraitist of the region. The mahogany, maple, and pine side chair, ca. 1750, has a pierced heart in the splat. On the stair landing are eighteenth-century cabinetmaker's samples—a slant-front desk and a side chair. The shelf clock was made between 1785 and 1795 by David Wood of Newburyport, Massachusetts.

Finishing Touches

The first chapter, Colonial Styles, like the other five chapters in *Decorating with Americana*, concludes with a feature called Finishing Touches. Here we provide examples of reproduction furniture and furnishings. Interior-design consulting editor Alexandra Stoddard also adds a decorating idea or two for each period. Throughout the book, when a period reproduction is illustrated, a reference number (e.g., R.G. #61) is included in the caption to refer readers to the listing of manufacturers in the book's Resource Guide (pages 208–217).

About Period Reproductions

The increasing popularity of genuine American antiques has created a diminishing supply of affordable, good quality eighteenth-, nineteenth-, and even early-twentieth-century furniture and accessories. The results have been not only steadily rising prices at auctions and in dealers' showrooms but also the increasing acceptance of quality reproduction furniture. Since the 1876 centennial celebration of our independence, furniture manufacturers have been reviving Colonial and early-nineteenth-century styles. But what is perhaps the most dramatic reproduction program was launched in 1937 by the Colonial Williamsburg Foundation. Since that time close to 3000 pieces, ranging from furniture to blazer buttons, have been reproduced from the Williamsburg Collection. The Foundation takes great care in the licensing of top manufacturers to faithfully reproduce from their 100,000-plus collection of antiques. Their offerings are in three categories: *Reproductions* are copies of original pieces as precise as modern technology can produce; *Adaptations* are as carefully crafted as Reproductions, but have been altered slightly (in fabrics or wallpaper, for example, a documented original may be reproduced in several color options); *Interpretations* include furniture of modern construction or electrified items.

Among the other institutions that have followed Williamsburg's lead in offering top-quality reproductions are the Winterthur Museum, New York's Metropolitan Museum of Art, Historic Charleston, Historic Savannah, Old Sturbridge Village, Boston's Museum of Fine Arts, and Shakertown at Pleasant Hill, Kentucky.

While Williamsburg Reproductions are often associated with high-style furniture—Queen Anne, Chippendale—last year this handsome country bow-back Windsor armchair was added to their extensive catalog [R.G. #229].

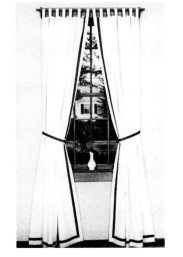

Tab curtains were used in Plymouth and other colonies from the earliest days. Illustrated here is a pair in natural muslin with grosgrain ribbon borders. Constance Carol, Inc. [R.G. #251] of Plymouth, Massachusetts, also carries a variety of hand-stencil-bordered tab curtains and others in the Colonial style.

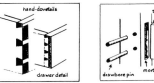

In addition to museums, the high art of quality reproduction craftsmanship is increasingly being practiced by small- and medium-sized firms throughout the country. A prime example is the Massachusetts firm of Simms and Thayer [R.G. #161], makers of the Connecticut cupboard, ca. 1780, illustrated *below*. The precision with which they finish their furniture can be seen in their use of hand-cut dovetails in drawers and pegged mortise-and-tenon construction in the joinings of their splendid country pieces.

The Rococo design of this Metropolitan Museum of Art [R.G. #220] sterling-silver reproduction sugar tongs, *below*, is characteristic of the time of the original's making, ca. 1765.

Hurley Patentee Manor [R.G. #192] creates handcrafted sconces, lamps, and chandeliers based on original seventeenth-, eighteenth-, and nine-teenth-century lighting fixtures in museums and private collections. Illustrated *above* is its all-tin, twelve-branched chandelier, "The Flowing Fountain." Available for candles or electrified.

R.W. Alexander, a master cabinetmaker in Lakeville, Connecticut, who calls his shop "Yes-terday's Yankee" [R.G. #169], crafts Colonial furniture and accessories in kiln-dried pine that are faithful in style to the originals but "not slavish...incorporating technical improvements in workmanship and materials." The original of this seventeenth-century coved cupboard, *above,* was made in Rhode Island.

This silver-plate beaker is a faithful reproduction of an original made by Myer Myers of New York in the period 1760–1795. It is available from Winterthur [R.G. #230].

56

Need an ancestor? If you have a home decorated in the Colonial manner and do not happen to have portraits of your eighteenth-century ancestors in hand, here are two alternatives: Winterthur [R.G. #230] offers a gold-framed reproduction portrait of young Benjamin Tevis, painted in 1822. Or, if you prefer familial faces, A. Strader Folk Art Co. [R.G. #162] will paint likenesses of your children in the costumes of earlier times, using the technique appropriate to the period.

The garden bench and planter boxes illustrated are Historic Charleston [R.G. #140] reproduc-tions from Thomas Chippendale designs. The wood is treated with preservative, then under-coated and sprayed with an exterior oil-base enamel.

Only the most prosperous Americans in Colonial times had the luxury of carpeted floors, but paintings of the period show Turkish carpets, such as this Transylvanian prayer rug, in Colonial homes. Williamsburg has reproduced this hand-some rug, the original of which is on display in the Governor's Palace at Colonial Williamsburg *(see the room view opposite).*

Museum houses illustrated in this chapter that are open to the public (contact the museums for hours) are:

Gunston Hall
U.S. 1
Lorton, Virginia 22079
703-550-9220

Stanley-Whitman House
37 High Street
Farmington, Connecticut 06032
203-677-9222

Colonial Williamsburg
Visitors' Center
Williamsburg, Virginia 23185
804-229-1000

Opposite: Every object in this cozy parlor at Williamsburg's Craft House [R.G. #229] is a faithful reproduction of an object in the Colonial Williamsburg collections.

The Federal Styles 1784–1815

The Nathaniel Russell house, *left,* is a beautifully appointed museum house of the Historic Charleston Foundation. It was built in 1808 by Russell, who had amassed a fortune in shipping from the South's busiest and most cosmopolitan port city. The house is modeled on the architectural style of the Scottish brother architects Robert and James Adam. In America this style is termed Federal. *Above:* A classic Southern walnut huntboard, an American Federal adaptation of the English Hepplewhite style (ca. 1790–1810). The blue and white tureen is Chinese Export (ca. 1800); the brass candlesticks are ca. 1740.

"The American war is over, but that is far from being the case with the American Revolution." These words were written in 1787 by Benjamin Rush, a distinguished Philadelphia physician and signer of the Declaration of Independence.

His prophecy proved to be all too true. The confederation of states formed in 1781 would not be united under a national constitution until 1789, and the young republic would come close to destruction at the hands of her former mother country in the War of 1812. In fact, national unity proved to be a very fragile thing until after the Civil War.

While the young country was struggling to gain its economic independence from England, London was to remain the style capital for Americans until the War of 1812.

Three British craftsmen were significant tastemakers for American architects, cabinetmakers, and

The architect for the Russell house, who is not known, observed an established Charleston custom when he placed the formal drawing room, *left,* on the second (i.e., ground-level) floor with windows that open on three sides to the garden, the street, and the sea air. As late as 1857, when Russell's heirs sold the house, it was still being described as "beyond all comparison, the finest establishment in Charleston." *Above:* A fine example of elegant interior detail is this grouping around a fireplace in Lake Erie Hall, in the Winterthur Museum. The lolling, or Martha Washington, chairs are ca. 1795; the porcelain objects on the mantel and in the wall cupboard are Chinese Export wares.

their clients. Robert Adam, a Scottish architect, had since the 1760s been incorporating classical—Greek and particularly Roman —design motifs into interior decorations and furniture designs. Like the Louis XVI style in France, Adam's designs incorporated classical elements such as urns and garlands. And late in the eighteenth century, Adam's concepts were popularized in furniture-design books by George Hepplewhite and Thomas Sheraton. American craftsmen were quick to utilize these design books and freely adapted both the Hepplewhite and Sheraton styles for the American market.

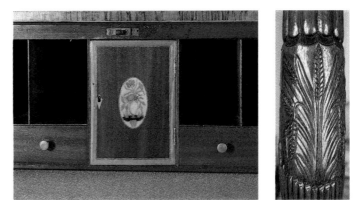

Four of the leading centers of manufacture of high-style Federal furniture in the early eighteenth century were Baltimore, Philadelphia, Boston, and Charleston. *Opposite:* A formal Federal parlor at the Winterthur Museum, near Wilmington, Delaware, incorporates a spectacular eagle-topped secretary, a cabriole sofa, and two small tables made in Baltimore or Philadelphia; a lolling chair made in Boston; and two pieces from South Carolina—the Pembroke tea table in the foreground and the side chair at the secretary. *Above:* A Charleston mahogany-veneered tambour desk of the same period is beautifully inlaid with satinwood, as seen in the detail *above middle.* The desk is in the Joseph Manigault house of the Charleston Museum. The Charleston bedroom in the Manigault house, *right,* contains a Federal period high-post "rice bed" with distinctive carvings of rice stalks on the posts *(see detail above right)* and intricate satinwood inlay on the crowning cornice. The headboard is removable, to allow freer circulation of air in the sultry summer months.

Charleston's prosperity in the late eighteenth and early nineteenth centuries is evidenced today by the surprisingly large number of private homes containing museum-quality furniture, such as that in the lovely dining room on the *opposite page.* The Federal-period furniture in this room has been handed down in the owner's family for many generations. The ancestor portraits of the late eighteenth and early nineteenth century attest to this continuity. *Below left:* This handsome Hepplewhite-style sideboard of the Federal period, of birch and walnut inlay, was made in Georgia, ca. 1800–1810. *Below:* Made of walnut with drawer fronts veneered in tiger maple, this Kentucky huntboard now graces a Birmingham, Alabama, home. Part of the owner's collection of Meissen porcelain is displayed on the wall above.

With the advent of trade between the United States and China in 1784, a rich new influence was introduced into American decorative arts. In that year the sailing ship *The Empress of China* left the port of New York for the 188-day voyage to Canton, China. The outgoing cargo was ginseng root—a medicinal herb prized in the Orient. On the return voyage, the Chinese exports, in turn, included tea, silk, and chinaware. The beautiful Chinese porcelain almost immediately became the most coveted tableware for prosperous Americans.

The years 1783–1815, termed the "Federal period" in our decorative-arts history, were a time of dramatic change in the tastes and life-styles of Americans, particularly in those of the growing number of affluent Americans. In urban centers along the East Coast prosperous businessmen were building restrained and elegant town houses such as the Nathaniel Russell house (page 58).

64

Nantucket Island, off Massachusetts, is in many ways a self-contained architectural museum. The oldest house dates from the early seventeenth century, and a remarkable number of homes in the Colonial, Federal, and Greek Revival styles remain, many with original furnishings. The furnishings remain largely because, after the whaling industry died down in the mid-nineteenth century (when whale oil was replaced by other oils for lighting), the original inhabitants could not afford to redo their houses in the successions of new styles. *Left:* This nineteenth-century cedar-shingled cottage, seen through its hedge gate, may well have been a whaler's home. *Above:* In a corner of this informal library, shorebird decoys grace the table-top beneath a colorful hooked rug entitled "Tom and Dick." A stoneware table lamp with a homespun shade sits in front of a window adorned with the charming hallmark of this house—an interior flower box filled with bright red geraniums. *Opposite:* Converted stoneware jugs topped with homespun shades make handsome lamps for the living room. A three-legged "cricket" table serves as side table near the couch, and an English camphorwood chest functions nicely as a coffee table. The stoneware pots on the bookshelf accent the collection of antique curlew decoys.

Right: In the library of this Nantucket house, a 1780 American pine desk and a nineteenth-century sack-back Windsor chair stand under an American primitive portrait, ca. 1830. A Boston fireboard, used in the nineteenth century to control room drafts when the fireplace was empty, hangs above an eighteenth-century American pine mantel. Two decoys face the Nantucket Lightship basket that sits between them. Two nineteenth-century metal Hessian soldier andirons stare over at another English camphorwood chest/coffee table, which adds to the house's charming design continuity.

Although splendid dining rooms like the Charleston room (page 65) were not uncommon in great houses in Europe, a separate dining room came as an innovation to the Federal period. With the more specific use of rooms, new furniture forms were required. The sideboard was one innovation introduced in this period. It served both as a storage piece for wine and utensils and as a serving table. Large extension or sectional dining tables were also introduced, replacing the smaller tilt-top and drop-leaf tables of earlier periods. The worktable, a small, graceful storage piece, and the Martha Washington chair, an upholstered piece with wooden arms, were other interesting new American forms.

The Hepplewhite and Sheraton designs within the Federal style period in this country had much in common: a neoclassical use of urns, swags, feathers, flowers, and our national bird, the eagle, in both carving and inlays; a lightness in construction (for mobility as well as style); and much emphasis on reeding, veneering, and painted decoration. Differences included designs of chair backs and legs: Hepplewhite emphasized heart-shaped backs and straight, tapered legs, whereas Sheraton utilized heavier forms, stressing square backs and round legs.

As illustrated in the room views that follow, new creative centers sprang up during this period: Salem in Massachusetts and Baltimore to the south are examples.

And, far to the Southwest, a rich Hispanic tradition was taking root. Santa Fe, founded in 1610, is the second oldest continuously inhabited city in the United States. (St. Augustine, Florida, was established in 1565.)

The classical look can be seen in all aspects of home furnishings in the period. *(See, for example, the classical window treatments in "Finishing Touches: In the Federal Manner" on pages 87–89.)*

This Nantucket dining room contains a wonderfully eclectic mix of antiques and crafts from three continents. *Above:* A lovely French oval fruitwood table is set with Canton china candlesticks and twentieth-century wineglasses from Providence, Rhode Island. Surrounding the table are four ''birdcage'' Windsor chairs, ca. 1810. An eighteenth-century copper rooster, flanked by two French pewter candlesticks, stands perched on the windowsill behind an 1890 American pine table. The portrait of the young woman which hangs in the corner is the work of an unknown artist from Massachusetts. *Opposite:* An American country-painted corner cupboard filled with Canton china is tucked away near the fireplace. On the mantel are candlesticks fashioned from wooden bobbins. Sitting under the folk-art painting by an unknown artist is a wooden broadbill duck decoy. The two wooden shorebirds on the French country-kitchen side table were crafted by Pat Gardner, a well-known native Nantucket carver. Here a black ''tall-chair'' Windsor heads the dining table. *Left:* A painting by Canadian artist David Bryan-Holmes hangs behind a bouquet of Queen Anne's lace arranged in a Spode china bowl.

Above: In a second-floor bedroom with two views of Nantucket Sound we see a reproduction of a nineteenth-century four-poster bed covered by a colorful quilt found in Nantucket. Lying between the English camphor-wood chest and the cricket bedside table is a nineteenth-century hooked rug by an unknown craftsman entitled "Playing with Pompey," which depicts a young girl playing with her dog. The geranium quilt hanging near the bay window seat is the work of local craftswoman Maggie Meredith. *Right:* A late-nineteenth-century quilt and an overshot coverlet, ca. 1825, from the Tennessee State Museum at Nashville. *Opposite:* A child's toy rocking horse, mounted on a wooden stand and set on top of a nineteenth-century painted bench, makes a lovely country sculpture for the hallway. Adding color to the space is an early-twentieth-century Amish quilt purchased at auction in New York.

This cozy Nantucket room, *above right,* serves as an overflow guest room as well as an office for its owners. The built-in cupboard bed has storage space above and below. The trunk and the basket beside the drop-front Victorian desk were purchased on the island. *Above:* This early-nineteenth-century maple tall-post bedstead is branded A. Shore,

probably of Somerset, Massachusetts. *Below:* These eight nesting baskets, late nineteenth or early twentieth century in origin, are Nantucket Lightship baskets, woven by sailors in the long hours aboard floating lighthouses anchored off the island.

Above: This Piedmont room at Winston-Salem's Museum of Early Southern Decorative Arts contains "back country" furnishings of the early 1800s, as would a simple frontier home—one room with sleeping loft above. The walnut table, the desk, and the bookcase were made in North Carolina, ca. 1770–1800. The side chair in the foreground is Virginia-made and country Chippendale in style. *Left:* A painted and grained linen chest from New England, ca. 1800–1815.

The dining room of a Nantucket house, *top*, contains an attractive mix of high-style and country furniture of the early nineteenth century. The sideboard is Federal period Hepplewhite in style; the table, also American, is Sheraton style of the same period. The painted chairs, probably from Connecticut, are ca. 1830. *Right:* This handsome painted Federal chair was made in Baltimore, a design center renowned for its richly painted and decorated furniture of this period. *Above:* This painted tinware, ca. 1815–1825, is from Pennsylvania, where German-American craftsmen also excelled in "freehand" painting and stenciling. The most elaborately decorated tinware is called toleware.

Left: This handsomely inlaid Sheraton-style china cabinet was made in Tennessee or Kentucky in the early 1800s. Located in Chattanooga's Houston Antique Museum, the cabinet contains pieces from the museum's extraordinary collection of porcelain and earthenware. *Above left:* This drop-leaf Sheraton dining room table was made in Boston, ca. 1805–1815. *Above:* This "grandfather" or tall-case clock, made in New England in the early nineteenth century, is considered a beautiful example of American folk art because of its original grain paint, the splendid eagle on its dial, and its original maple wood works.

Above right: This tilt-top table is seen in the dining room at Arlington, a Greek-Revival-style museum house in Birmingham, Alabama. The Federal piece from the North Carolina Piedmont is notable for its fine satinwood inlay decoration. Two other distinctive Southern pieces are the Virginia candlestand, *above,* with unusual turning and legs, and the Louisiana lolling chair, *right,* sometimes called a "planter's chair" or "boot jack chair." (The tired planter is said to have lolled back in his chair and raised his feet for assistance in removing his boots.)

78

Above left: The Federal-style mahogany butler's secretary, ca. 1810–1820, is notable for the intricate pineapple carving on its freestanding columns. *Above:* This walnut- and satinwood-inlaid slant-front desk is Southern in origin and was made in the early nineteenth century. *Left:* The classical form of this silver sauce dish is typical of early nineteenth-century taste. Its maker was Charles A. Burnet of Georgetown, District of Columbia.

Above: This contemporary adaptation of a Federal town house, in Spring Hill, Alabama, contains an eclectic collection of furnishings "edited down" when the owner moved from a larger house. *Right:* A small mahogany table made in the Salem, Massachusetts, area, ca. 1800, sits in the entrance hall. Its apron and top are inlaid with satinwood. The mirror, carved with acanthus leaves in the Federal manner, is ca. 1815. The brass lamp, now electric, has been converted from an early oil lamp, with its wick snuffer and scissors still attached. The miniatures and small watercolors add interest to the entrance. *Top:* An early-nineteenth-century Federal worktable. The bag contained wool and sewing implements.

Above: A North Carolina cellarette with two gin bottles of the early nineteenth century. *Left:* A corner cupboard from Virginia, ca. early nineteenth century.

Above left: A Contemporary Federal-style frame house in Alabama. The focal point of the living room, *below left,* is the carved Federal mantel salvaged from a New Bern, North Carolina, house built in 1805. On either side of the mantel are mahogany card tables of Massachusetts origin, ca. 1800. *Above:* A closer view of the handsome table with graceful Hepplewhite legs. The mahogany box contains a liqueur set. *Opposite:* The library/family room in the house also has attractive architectural details. It is paneled in native Alabama cypress. The prints above the settee are from McKenny and Hall's *History of the Indian Tribes of North America,* and include a portrait of Macintosh, a chief from the Mobile area. The chair with a pierced back slat is American, late eighteenth century. The bannister-back chair is probably British.

These handsome three-mold blown tumblers are copies of originals from the early nineteenth century. They are available through the Metropolitan Museum of Art [R.G. #220].

Below: This elegant sideboard, or side table, is from Winterthur Museum Reproductions [R.G. #230]. The original was made in Charleston, ca. 1790–1810.

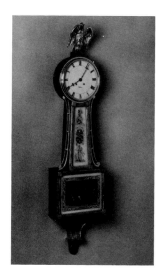

Above: A twenty-two-carat gold eagle tops this stylish banjo clock from Williamsburg Reproductions [R.G. #229]. It illustrates America's love of patriotic adornment at the time the original clock was made, in the early nineteenth century, in Boston. Its highly decorative case includes reverse painting on glass.

After the American Revolution, the French fashions in home furnishings were extremely popular. This late-eighteenth-century French wallpaper, ca. 1798–1799, has been faithfully reproduced by Brunschwig & Fils [R.G. #233]. The pattern is called "Bosquet."

Styles in window treatments—hanging curtains and draperies—have evolved throughout the history of decorative arts in America. Several of the catalogs of reproductions offered by museums give very helpful guidance. Shown *below* are two window treatments appropriate to the Federal style period, illustrated in the catalog of Historic Charleston Reproductions [R.G. #140]. *Below left:* A formal Adam looped swag treatment. The design ascendancy in America of the Scottish Adam brothers was from approximately 1780 to 1810. The Regency valance is also based on an English window treatment of the early nineteenth century.

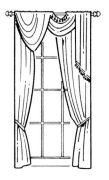 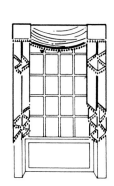

Museum houses illustrated in this chapter that are open to the public (contact the museums for hours) are:

Winterthur
The Henry Francis du Pont Winterthur Museum
Route 52
Winterthur, Delaware 19735
302-654-1548

Russell House
51 Meeting Street
Charleston, South Carolina 29401
803-723-1623

Joseph Manigault House
360 Meeting Street
Charleston, South Carolina 29403
803-722-2996

Museum of Early Southern Decorative Arts
924 South Main Street
Winston-Salem, North Carolina 27108
919-722-6148

Opposite: This beautifully crafted Charleston rice bed is made by Baker Furniture for the Historic Charleston Foundation. [R.G. #140]

The American Empire Style 1816–1840

Opposite: Edgewater, which sits majestically on the banks of the Hudson River, is a wonderful example of Neoclassical or Greek Revival architecture. Built about 1820 by John Robert Livingston for his daughter Margaret and son-in-law Lowndes Brown, the house was purchased in 1852 by Robert Donaldson, for whom Alexander Jackson Davis designed the octagonal library wing, visible at the left, in 1854. Robert and Susan Donaldson left many pieces of furniture, which the current owner, a dedicated collector, has been fortunate in tracking down and reinstalling in the house. *Above:* The rich mahogany and satinwood slant-front desk in the sitting room of Edgewater is attributed to Duncan Phyfe of New York City. Above it hangs a portrait of John Peter Van Ness by the early portraitist Gilbert Stuart.

During the War of 1812, the young American republic came perilously close to being overwhelmed and subjugated by the British crown. Had England's attentions not been diverted by a simultaneous power struggle with Napoleonic France, America might not have successfully prevailed over her former mother country. The years that followed the close of the war and the signing of the Treaty of Ghent, in 1815, encompassed a new era that has often been referred to by historians as the "age of expansion." It was expansive in all aspects of American activity and consciousness, not only in geography (in 1803 the size of the country had doubled with the Louisiana Purchase) but in education, science, transportation, and the arts. For the first time a generation of citizens came of age in unturbulent times. In such a period Americans found the opportunity to turn inward and direct their energies toward such achievements as the exploration of their uncharted land; the building of major roads to connect the cities of the East and foster the settlement of the West; the completion of the Erie

Above: The sofa and worktable at the right in the Edgewater library were made for Robert Donaldson by the well-known New York cabinetmaker Duncan Phyfe, probably in 1822. Of a contemporary date is the extremely large New York pier table at the right. Above it stands a portrait of John Craythorne Montgomery, painted by Jacob Eichholtz in about 1830. The armchairs flanking the fireplace and the center table are also New York Empire pieces. The carpet was made recently to the designs of William Thompson, who drew on a ceiling decoration in Pompeii as his source. *Right:* The American bookcase in the library of Edgewater is one of a pair; it dates from about 1830. On it is a plaster copy of a bust of John Paul Jones executed by Jean Antoine Houdon, a French sculptor who captured the likenesses of many eminent Americans. To the right is a portrait of Mrs. Cornelius Schuyler painted by Abel Buel Moore about 1840. The marble bust of Julius Caesar at left was carved in the early nineteenth century.

Right: This pier table in rosewood veneer, with gilt-winged supports and dolphin feet, is attributed to Charles-Honoré Lannuier, New York, ca. 1835. *Above right:* A pier table made in New York about 1815 and attributed to Duncan Phyfe stands in the elegant entrance hall of Edgewater. The looking glass over the pier table descended in the Ten Eyck family of Albany, New York; it dates from the early nineteenth century. The nineteenth-century English vase on the table is said to have belonged to Robert and Susan Donaldson. At the end of the hall is a lyre-base card table made in New York in the early nineteenth century. The portrait above it, by an unknown artist, is thought to depict Sarah Bond Ion Lowndes of Charleston, South Carolina. The carved and gilded wall brackets on either side were made in New York or Albany about 1820. The floor, painted in a stylized nineteenth-century design, was executed by Robert Jackson in 1980. *Above:* This richly carved and gilded girandole mirror, ca. 1820, is thought to be of Philadelphia origin.

Canal, to strengthen our waterway system; and then the further uniting of the vast land through the building of railroads.

It was an innovative time in the decorative arts as well, and it gave rise to a new style that is called Greek Revival in architecture and "Empire" in the plastic arts. Although the term Empire connotes a style that was popularized in France, the style was actually rooted in the ancient civilizations of Egypt and classical antiquity—a past with which our young democracy idealistically and fervently identified. There was a close adherence to actual objects that archaeologists had excavated at the sites of ancient Greek and Roman cities and through Napoleon's military campaigns in Egypt in 1798 and 1799. Two examples are the Baltimore-made klismos chair (*see page 110*), with its saber legs, canted

back, and curved crest rail (which has a direct antecedent in chairs made in Greece in the fifth century B.C.), and the curule chair, with its rounded, X-shaped base (which enjoyed widespread usage in ancient Rome).

Above: Edgewater's north bedroom is appointed with French-inspired Empire pieces made in New York between 1820 and 1840. The large secretary on the left-hand wall is attributed to Joseph Meeks & Sons, New York City cabinetmakers. *Right:* This commode (washstand) with gilt stencil decoration is of New York manufacture, ca. 1830. *Above right:* This vitrine (wardrobe) is of Neoclassical—or Empire—style, possibly French, ca. 1820.

In their style preferences Americans turned away from England and looked to France as a center. One reason was that Americans were politically disposed to the French following the War of 1812 and were still appreciative of their support during the American Revolution. (This admiration was nationally recognized when the Marquis de Lafayette, French hero of the American Revolution, was invited to make a triumphal tour of the United States in 1824 and 1825.) Another, more specific, factor was that French design books had become available to American craftsmen, many of whom were French immigrants.

Above middle: This American-made "sleigh bed" in the Conde-Charlotte bedroom, American Empire in style, may have been manufactured in New Orleans. The canopy on the wall above the bed is a French decorating detail of the 1830s. *Above right:* In an old New England farmhouse, a unique Neoclassical effect has been created with a sleigh bed, a Roman bust, and a ficus tree. *Below left:* Possibly French, this Empire mahogany toilet table is of the nineteenth century. *Below:* This handsome ladies' worktable was made in Boston, ca. 1815–1820. *Above left:* In the American Empire bedroom in Mobile's Conde-Charlotte house is displayed a period dressing table on which sits a looking glass within a frame decorated with swans' heads.

Above: Traveler's Rest, a historic museum house in Nashville, houses this handsome American Empire-style bedroom. The room contains several furniture forms in the "French taste," popular in New Orleans. The lolling chair upholstered in red leather, ca. 1830, is executed in a form often termed a Spanish chair or planter's chair (Thomas Jefferson is known to have ordered several from New Orleans for his home at Monticello). The armoire is from New Orleans, ca. 1830. *Below:* A brass-decorated rosewood game table in the Empire style made in New York, possibly by the shop of Duncan Phyfe, the renowned Scottish-American cabinetmaker.

Although figural carving was not a prominent feature in furniture design of the Federal period, it became an important element of the Empire style. Heads, legs, and paws drawn from a large bestiary of both real and mythological creatures were carved as supports for chairs, tables, sofas, and other pieces. Favored decorative devices were those of dolphins, swans, eagles, lions, dogs, rams, and fantastical mermaids, caryatids, and griffins.

Along with this furniture of slightly heavier proportions came deeper carving and more elaborate ornamentation, often in the form of stenciling, grain painting, gilding, and applied ormolu mounts. New forms also emerged: the sleigh bed, pier tables with mirrored backs, recamier sofas, and the convex looking-glass are a few. The scale and form of neoclassically inspired furniture were particularly harmonious with the high ceilings and symmetrically proportioned rooms both in Southern plantations constructed during the antebellum period and in grand houses, in the form of Greek temples, like Edgewater, on the Hudson River (*see page 90*).

Perhaps the most famous craftsman working within the late Federal and early Empire styles was Scottish-born Duncan Phyfe. His thriving business operated in New York City (which had become a style center) between 1795 and 1847. Not so much an innovator of design, Phyfe proved to be a master of adaptation—first of the English Sheraton and Regency styles (up to about 1815) and later of the French Empire style, which catered to the increasingly cosmopolitan and international tastes of his clients throughout the East Coast. Phyfe was the first American cabinetmaker to make klismos and curule chairs.

Two other craftsmen advanced the designs of the Empire period, and both were French emigrés: Charles-Honoré Lannuier, who also worked in New York City between 1803 and 1819, and Anthony G. Quervelle, who was active in Philadelphia around 1817 to 1856. Both worked in a modified French style. Indicative of these craftsmen's success as arbiters of taste is Quervelle's making of two pier tables for the White House in the late 1820s, and Dolley Madison's reputed ordering of furniture from Lannuier.

Domestic manufacturers had thrived since the first decade of the century, when Jefferson's acts of embargo restricted trade with European countries and brought greater attention to American-made goods. Foundries produced more and more utilitarian and decorative metalwares in iron and brass, and glassworks and textile mills were also established in several New England states. The first successful porcelain works, the Tucker China Factory, was founded in Philadelphia in 1825, and by the early 1830s there were more and more Americans who wanted and could afford furnishings that were more than basically utilitarian.

Left: The living room of a Mobile town house is furnished with American antiques of several styles. The tray-top cherry tea table is Connecticut Queen Anne, ca. 1730. The mahogany-veneered sofa is pillar-and-scroll American Empire, ca. 1840. The carved mahogany tilt-top table to the left of the sofa is ca. 1825. The gilt mirror above, ca. 1815–1820, is in the Sheraton style. The large mahogany bookcase, ca. 1835, contains a collection of pewter. *Below:* A New York center, or drum, table is of the early Neoclassical period. *Above:* The Georgian dining room at the Winterthur Museum has been re-created from a Milledgeville, Georgia, house of the 1830s.

Above right: In Madame John's Legacy, a Louisiana State Museum house in New Orleans, a parlor is furnished with Louisiana furniture. The sofa and chairs, ca. 1830, are probably from the workshop of François Seignoret, a noted local cabinetmaker. *Above:* An escritoire (writing desk), ca. 1835, in the Napoleon Room of Mobile's Conde-Charlotte house. *Below:* This type of Empire couch is called a recamier. This example, crafted in mahogany and inlaid brass, was made in New York, ca. 1815–1820.

Above right: A prosperous merchant erected this handsome Greek-Revival-style town house in 1830 near Greenwich Village in New York City. *Above left:* The interior has been faithfully restored as a museum house and is open to the public. This view shows the two parlors on the "first" floor (upstairs from street level), with gondola chairs, ca. 1830, in the foreground. On the mantel are Argand gas lamps (a French invention, named for their creator); a pair of the single-globe variety called Astral lamps are seen *below left. Below:* A gondola chair, ca. 1830, attributed to the Seignoret workshop.

Below right: Another fine example of the symmetrical Greek Revival style in architecture is the Bartow-Pell Mansion, built in Pelham Bay Park, New York City, between 1836 and 1842. *Right:* This exquisite free-standing spiral staircase in the front hall of the mansion sweeps from the ground floor to the attic. The rich plaster ornamentation above the doors, on the ceiling cornice, and in the ceiling rosette is particularly noteworthy. Early-nineteenth-century New York pieces include the mahogany card table and the center table, which has rich ormolu mounts and gilding characteristic of Empire furniture. The dolphin arm supports seen on the armchair, which is French, ca. 1820, are a feature of both French and American Empire styles. The Savonnerie rug is French, made between 1820 and 1830. *Below left:* In the library of the mansion is an American mahogany and mahogany-veneered sofa. The painting above the sofa, executed in 1853 by Louis Lang, is entitled *The Basket Maker*. *Opposite:* The richly carved and gilded furniture in the drawing room is a fitting accompaniment to the ornate plasterwork. The stencil-decorated pier table on the left-hand wall was probably made in New York, ca. 1815. Also of New York manufacture is the early-nineteenth-century pianoforte, labeled by John Geib and Sons, with works by Robert and William Nunns. The elaborately carved and gilded girandole mirror is probably American, ca. 1820. The window hangings are adapted from designs in George Smith's *Cabinet-maker and Upholsterer's Guide and Repository of Designs*, published in London in 1826.

Left: In a Connecticut cottage parlor, a Neoclassical mantel mirror, ca. 1830, reflects ancestor portraits and other artifacts of the period. A brightly stenciled Hitchcock chair and an English folding campaign-chair, both ca. 1830, are among the room's furnishings. *Right:* A green-painted and gold-stenciled "Baltimore" chair, early nineteenth century. *Above:* A more formal Neoclassical library adorned with a glass chandelier and a child's rocker.

By the end of the 1830s the graceful straight lines and vigorous, crisp carving characteristic of the early Empire period were supplanted by designs that relied on much heavier components—plain, solid surfaces composed of exotic woods, flat scrolls, and massive columns. This pillar-and-scroll furniture, as it is often called, was typically mass-produced with a band saw (invented in 1840) and veneered in mahogany, walnut, or rosewood. The impact of this technological innovation has been accurately assessed by Russell Lynes in his book *The Tastemakers:* "Suddenly almost everybody, instead of just a wealthy and cultured few, could buy 'tasteful' carpets and chairs, wallpapers and curtain materials."

The country kitchen, *above*, is in an 1840s addition to an earlier house in northwestern Connecticut. The present owners raised the ceiling and converted three small rooms into one cooking and serving space. The table and side chairs are from Pennsylvania, ca. 1825. Folk art decoys and a painting of the early twentieth century, and copperware, stoneware, and baskets of the nineteenth century are seen on the walls and cabinets. *Left:* In the same kitchen a Pennsylvania corner cupboard, ca. 1825, contains a collection of Chinese Export dinnerware and American pewter. Atop the cupboard is displayed a tin model of the clipper ship *David McKay* of Boston, possibly crafted by one of the ship's party during one of the clipper's trips to the Orient in the 1840s.

Above: In a modern addition to a nineteenth-century cottage, the owners have combined old and new. The pine beds are ca. 1830s; the New England Windsor chairs are early nineteenth century; the quilt and appliquéd coverlets are late-nineteenth-century family pieces. The contemporary carpeting, small-pattern wallpaper, and curtains are in earth tones that complement the older furnishings. Also of the Hitchcock style are these painted washstands, *right.* Before indoor plumbing, every bedroom contained a similar piece to accommodate a washbasin and pitcher.

Right: In the first half of the nineteenth century in America, few country families could afford the walnut-, mahogany-, or rosewood-veneered furniture favored by urban homeowners. But native woods could be painted —in ways that simulated the grains of the richer woods, or with stenciling or freehand painting. The beautifully painted primitive Connecticut chest has landscapes adorning the drawer fronts. *Above:* This large, black, American Empire-style bureau, ca. 1840–1850, attributed to Lambert Hitchcock, is handsomely stenciled. *Above right:* In these charming 1836 watercolors, a New England couple in their Sunday best are seated on painted and stenciled chairs of the period.

One such innovator in the realm of mass-production techniques in furniture making was Lambert Hitchcock, of Hitchcocksville (now Riverton), Connecticut. The gaily painted and gilded stenciled chairs he produced as early as 1825 are today considered quintessential forms of the period. Although they owe much in overall design to the English Sheraton style, these so-called fancy chairs embody all the exuberance of an industrializing America.

The handsome brick structure *above* was built as a residence in 1820 but creatively restored in 1981 as a branch office for the Monroe Savings Bank of Rochester, New York. The interior of the bank, *opposite page*, is filled with nineteenth-century cupboards, side chairs, and tables, and even contains two continuous-arm eighteenth-century Windsor chairs. Desks were custom-made from old wood found in the attic, and the walls have been charmingly stenciled with eagles, tulips, leaves, and pots of flowers. *Above right:* This American Empire mahogany armchair, made in New York ca. 1835, has deeply carved legs. Its original upholstery—in need of repair—is green leather.

Other manufacturers produced a number of innovations. Eli Terry, for example, was a Connecticut clockmaker who devised an inexpensive wooden movement in place of the usual metal one. He did this in partnership with another ingenious Connecticut Yankee, Seth Thomas, who also produced independently a variety of neo-classically inspired shelf clocks with cases that were unlike any made in Europe until that time. In order to safeguard such new designs, and to ensure uninfringeable profits, the patenting of furniture designs came into practice.

Reflective of a rise in national spirit was the incorporation of patriotic imagery in the decorative arts. The ubiquitous symbols of the Federal period—the flag and the eagle—were amplified to include portrait busts of our national heroes: Washington, Lafayette, Franklin, Andrew Jackson, and others. Their likenesses were emblazoned on metalwares, glass, ceramics, and textiles.

Above: This faithfully handcrafted reproduction of a nineteenth-century country piece—a pie safe with punched tin doors and solid pine construction—is a product of the Cabin Creek Furniture Company of Wake Forest, North Carolina [R.G. #121].

This watercolor—recently auctioned by Phillips, New York [R.G. #83]—was painted in the early 1800s. Titled "Bird, Fruit and Butterfly," it was executed on velvet by an anonymous artist. Original paintings of this quality often bring up to $1,500 at auction.

Below: This graceful armchair in the Neoclassical or Empire style is a Williamsburg Reproduction [R.G. #229] of an early-nineteenth-century English piece. The maker of the original updated his design, copied almost literally from that of an ancient Greek klismos chair, by caning the seat and back and painting the chair green.

Below: In Brompton, a Greek Revival house in Fredericksburg, Virginia, the window treatments in the parlor are swag-and-jabot draperies over cotton curtains, a popular American Empire treatment.

Museum houses illustrated in this chapter that are open to the public (contact the museums for hours) are:

Bartow-Pell Mansion
Pelham Bay Park
Bronx, New York 10464

Fort Conde-Charlotte House
104 Theatre Street
Mobile, Alabama 36602
205-432-4722

Old Merchant's House
29 East Fourth Street
New York, New York 10003
212-777-1089

The Brooklyn Museum
Eastern Parkway
Brooklyn, New York 11238
212-638-5000

Madame John's Legacy
632 Dumaine Street
New Orleans, Louisiana 70116

Winterthur
The Henry Francis du Pont Winterthur Museum
Route 52
Winterthur, Delaware 19735
302-654-1548

The John T. Kenney Museum
Hitchcock Chair Company
Riverton, Connecticut 06065
203-379-8531

Opposite: This room is completely furnished in Hitchcock reproductions. Founded in 1825, the Hitchcock Furniture Company of Riverton, Connecticut, is one of America's oldest and most respected furniture manufacturers [R.G. #141].

Victorian Styles 1841–1889

Opposite: This sprawling Victorian house in Columbus, Mississippi, incorporates design attributes of several nineteenth-century styles. Its mansard roof tower, arched windows, and ironwork suggest, however, that its style is closest to Second Empire (1860–1890), a style derived from French architecture and often followed in Mississippi and Louisiana.

Above: This grouping of Rococo Revival furniture (1845–1870) seen in the Conde-Charlotte house museum in Mobile, Alabama, includes a marble-topped center table, chairs, and an étagère (or whatnot), all of ornately carved mahogany.

In 1840, America's vast lands encompassed twenty-six states and a population of more than seventeen million. The industrial revolution made possible large-scale exploitation of a number of inventions that in turn had profound effects on American tastes, life-styles, and class consciousness.

The proliferation of the steamboat and the steam locomotive fostered an explosion of commercial enterprises. By midcentury, close to ten thousand miles of railroad track created a network connecting our eastern cities, and by 1869 there would be a transcontinental railroad. Homeowners across the land found it possible to obtain the latest styles in furniture and household accessories much more readily and at lower cost.

Agriculture was booming at midcentury, in part as a result of Cyrus McCormick's invention of the reaper. Communications, too, underwent enormous growth, through Samuel Morse's development of the telegraph in 1844. The transmission of news from our rapidly widening frontiers to our centers of industry and

Above: A ''turtle-top'' Rococo Revival table, attributed to John-Henry Belter of New York City, ca. 1850. *Right:* Original brocatelle draperies, French gilt mirrors, and a chandelier made in Philadelphia in 1845 grace this majestic drawing room in Melrose plantation at Natchez, Mississippi. Skillful carvings of scrolls and flowers adorn the original rosewood furniture. The reproduction carpet was expertly copied from a Rococo Revival remnant in another Natchez home.

government in the East contributed to the nation's development.

Conflict over what came to be known as the Tariff of Abominations, which protected northern industry and penalized southern planters and manufacturers, and the divisive issue of slavery brought forth the bloody Civil War that began in 1861, by which time eleven southern states had seceded from the Union. Much of the storied plantation life-style was lost with the defeat of the Confederacy, and many beautiful Colonial, Federal, and Greek Revival houses were destroyed in the war.

The years 1840 to 1890 saw tumultuous change in the political and commercial life of the nation, and this was reflected in the decorative arts, which were immensely affected by the trend toward modernization. National magazines such as *Harper's New Monthly* and *Godey's Lady's Book* did much to dictate and popularize current fashions and ''correct taste'' among an expanding middle class. Catalogs were issued by manufacturers throughout the country, bringing customers from faraway places and introducing innovations in style to all corners of the country.

Top right: Melrose, built in 1845, is an outstanding example of architecture in the Greek Revival style. Its portico, in which the large-scale Doric columns are spaced in a wide central bay with a narrower bay to each side, distinguishes it architecturally from all other mansions of its time. The main body of the house is constructed of red brick with Doric columns separating the entrance doorway from the sidelights. *Above:* One of the most dramatic rooms in Melrose is the dining room. The original furnishings include a table that can accommodate up to fourteen diners, fourteen Gothic Revival chairs, and a sideboard labeled "by Charles White of Philadelphia." The wool rug, made in Spain, is an original composite design from documented Empire designs. The meticulously carved mahogany punkah fan was moved by a servant to create a pleasant breeze on hot summer nights. *Above right:* A mahogany side chair of the Gothic Revival style, now on display at the Brooklyn Museum.

Books also played a major role in tastemaking. In 1840 John Hall, of Baltimore, published *The Cabinet Maker's Assistant*, which maintained the popularity of pillar-and-scroll-type furniture for decades, even as other styles emerged. And emerge they did, at a quickening pace. In his highly influential book of 1850, *The Architecture of Country Houses*, Andrew Jackson Downing praised the "Grecian or neoclassical style," but also advocated others: the Gothic Revival, the Elizabethan Revival, and the Rococo, or "French taste," as Downing labeled it. He warned against confusing "fashion" and "correct taste." The latter, he wrote, is "remarkable for agreeable and harmonious lines and forms and well adapted to its setting and function…not necessarily bright with gilding and rich with satin and velvet…which may be 'out of fashion'…in a twelvemonth."

Above: Two original four-poster mahogany tester beds sit upstairs in the master bedroom. The chest between the beds bears the label of Anthony G. Quervelle of Philadelphia. *Right:* Seen in the Winedale Inn Historic House of the University of Texas at Austin is this walnut full tester bed, ca. 1857.

In this stylistically eclectic period, it was not uncommon for a furniture warehouse to sell a parlor suite composed of several styles, with, for example, chairs in the Gothic style, a table in the Elizabethan mode, and a sofa of Rococo design.

New styles coexisted with those of an earlier age, and in some regions of the country—particularly outside the more sophisticated urban style centers—a specific method of design might be adopted late, or not at all. Thus, the dating of the various revival styles is by necessity approximate, and this list provides a guideline.

Gothic Revival	1840s
Elizabethan Revival	1850s on
Egyptian Revival	1850s–1860s
Rococo Revival	1850s–1900
Renaissance Revival	1850–1875
Louis XVI Revival	1860s–1870
Eastlake	1870–1880s
Japanese Revival	1876–1880s
Colonial Revival	1876–1920s

The Gothic style, which had been revived in England by A.W.N. Pugin in the 1830s, appeared in this country by the 1840s. It is most readily identified by its use of motifs such as pointed arches *(see the chair illustrated on page 118)* and pierced tracery, both typical of the medieval period.

The Elizabethan Revival style is characterized by the heaviness of English furniture of the sixteenth century. It usually incorporates ball-and-spiral turnings *(see page 121)*.

The French design vocabulary is evident in both the Rococo Revival furniture that appeared in the 1850s and 1860s and in the Renaissance Revival style that was popular between about 1850 and 1875. Rococo furniture is richly ornamented with carving, as is evident in the work of John-Henry Belter, perhaps the greatest proponent of the style *(see page 116)*. The most distinguished maker of Renaissance Revival furniture was the French emigré Leon Marcotte, among whose clients was the family of Theodore Roosevelt.

Top right: Arlington, an Alabama plantation in Birmingham, was built in Greek Revival style in the early 1840s. Its carefully restored rooms contain furnishings of several periods. The parlor, *above,* contains Rococo Revival pieces as well as a sofa of American Empire or Neoclassical style. The bedroom, *at right,* is in Rococo Revival style. The beautifully carved Rococo Revival slipper chair, *top left,* is attributed to John-Henry Belter of New York, regarded as the master furniture maker of that style.

Right: The Hanger House, an exuberantly decorated Victorian shingled dwelling in Little Rock, Arkansas, is in the Queen Anne architectural style. *Below:* The parlor in the Hanger House is as richly painted, wallpapered, and architecturally embellished as the exterior. The inlaid and ebonized wood table in the foreground is in Renaissance Revival style, ca. 1860. *Bottom right:* The platform rocker with spool-turned side supports is in Elizabethan Revival style, ca. 1883.

The battle of the styles, as one critic of the period has called it, continued throughout the century, as Americans rallied to A.J. Downing's urging that "we devote our life and humble efforts to raising the condition of the individual home." With so many design options being mass-produced, and thus reasonably priced, in such places as Grand Rapids, Michigan, no homeowner lacked opportunities for individual expressions of taste in the home.

Above: This exhibit room in the Brooklyn Museum is furnished in late Victorian styles. The armchair, *right,* is Renaissance Revival, ca. 1870–1880, made in Brooklyn. *Above right:* The wall clock, ca. 1875, was made by Connecticut's Ansonia Clock Company.

Right: This elaborate room, now in the Brooklyn Museum, was originally in John D. Rockefeller's New York brownstone, built in 1860 and remodeled in its Moorish style in 1885. By this period, wealthy Victorian Americans had seemingly revived all the styles of Western art and now began to borrow exotic motifs from the Orient and Near East.
Below: A bamboo maple desk in the Oriental style, ca. 1870.

Above left: An entrance hall at Melrose plantation is used as an office area, with a Victorian plantation desk on one wall and a secretary-bookcase on the other. *Above:* A Victorian oak hall-tree, a popular form in the late nineteenth century. *Top:* A nineteenth-century cast-iron umbrella stand in the form of a sailor working rope.

Above right: This elaborately carved walnut sideboard, ca. 1870–1880, is in the Renaissance Revival style. The Victorian silver pieces on its marble top include a Rococo water pitcher, on wheels, from Philadelphia.
Above: A walnut desk on chest of drawers, ca. 1860; it was made in Washington County, Texas.

Left: The elements of this bedroom show clearly the preference of the owners of this country weekend refuge. The painted Elizabethan Revival "cottage" furniture, which was highly praised by Victorian design arbiter Andrew Jackson Downing, has been left in "as found" condition. A painted box, a hooked rug, and a collection of straw hats complete a handsome still life. *Below:* A cottage-style dresser of the mid-nineteenth century. *Below left:* A crazy quilt made in Baltimore in the 1850s. These quilts were often called "friendship" quilts when the many varied-pattern patches were supplied by friends of the maker.

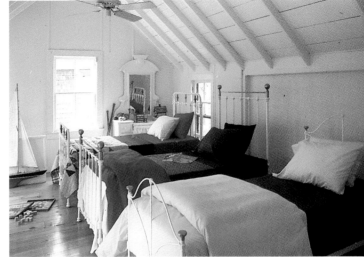

Right: In this summer beach house, the problem of how to bed varying numbers of unexpected young guests was solved by creating a children's dormitory in the attic. The walls and floors are left unadorned, the metal beds dressed in a rainbow of linens. *Below:* In this Victorian guest room, matching wallpaper and fabric has been used to excellent advantage. The small floral design is a flattering backdrop to the brass bed and wall-hung quilt (which incorporates the theme fabric). *Below right:* An electrified Victorian brass lamp complements a brass bedstead.

Opposite bottom: A charming private sunken garden behind a Savannah town house. The Rococo metal furniture, urns, and fountain are aluminum reproductions of Victorian pieces. *Opposite top left:* A lion head architectural detail salvaged from an earlier time. *Opposite top right:* Loving hands have clearly had their way with this farmhouse porch. The wicker rockers and planter, and an old-fashioned swing, are painted black to give emphasis to the vivid colors of the appliquéd pillows and table dress. *Above and left:* Victorian wicker furniture is the principal style element in these two guest bedrooms. Painted white, wicker provides a perfect background for colorful fabrics, wallcovering, and accessories. The period 1880–1890 was a high point in the popularity of wicker furniture. The rocker at left was probably made by the Heywood Brothers and Wakefield Company of Wakefield, Massachusetts, which in 1879 sold over two million dollars' worth of wicker furniture and accessories—an extraordinary figure considering that the average cost for a chair at the time was $3.

Left: This house in Lafayette, Louisiana, is new but its architect, A. Hayes Town, has used the styles and handcrafted details of nineteenth-century southern Louisiana and Mississippi. Supported by hand-hewn posts, the roof extends well beyond the front wall of the house to shelter the porch. *Below left:* A sturdy Louisiana Windsor chair, ca. 1850. *Below:* Architect Town has screened a service area off the garden with a wall of shutters.

Right: This toolshed on a Lafayette estate was designed in the form of a pigeonier (pigeon house), an outbuilding common in French Louisiana. *Below:* Hand-split shingles, old brick, and doors are featured in the design of another house by A. Hayes Town. *Below right:* A Neoclassical cast-iron urn and a cast-iron boot-scraper—both Victorian relics—grace the front steps of a Spring Hill, Alabama, house.

Below: A restored dog-trot log cabin in Dawes, Alabama. Log cabins have traditionally been built one-and-a-half stories high with a fireplace at one end—one room with a sleeping loft above. Log cabins were seldom more than sixteen feet by sixteen feet because logs longer than that were difficult to work with. One design that could provide additional space was the dog-trot, really two cabins with a common roof over a porch separating the cabins, through which a dog—and many other creatures—might trot. *Historic Preservation* wrote in its April 1984 cover story that "canny homeowners and professional restorers are transforming rustic 'derelict' cabins into 'country chic' retreats." *Right:* The decor of this hall in a Lookout Mountain, Tennessee, restored log cabin is a classic example of creative melding of styles. The painting is a 1926 N.C. Wyeth, the doorway is turn-of-the-century lead glass, and the painted chest is from Pennsylvania, ca. 1810.

Left: The owners of the Lookout Mountain log cabin are dedicated collectors. Here in a corner of their living room is a Pennsylvania painted cupboard, ca. 1810, containing an assortment of American folk art, including metal toys, carved wooden figures, and Navajo blankets. *Below:* A folk-art collectible that is increasingly popular is the hooked rug. This large rug is from Maine, ca. 1885.

Left and below: This restored dog-trot log cabin in Georgia was moved by its owners from Tennessee. The National Trust for Historic Preservation indicates that the first log cabins in America were built in the Delaware River basin by Swedish colonists in the sixteenth century. Restored cabins like this one in Georgia are classic showcases for country furniture and crafts, such as the baskets and rugs seen here. *Below left:* On a country cottage porch, an old kitchen chopping table is used as a side table next to a cane-backed Victorian rocker.

Below: The kitchen of the Georgia cabin seen on the preceding pages. *Below right:* In another simple, plank-walled kitchen, mid-nineteenth-century furniture—a Pennsylvania corner cupboard, pine table, and slat-back chairs—is accented with a converted brass gaslight lamp, a primitive wooden bowl, and a painting of a man at prayer. *Right:* An 1875 pie safe, a perennial favorite in country kitchens. The cupboard's doors are made of decoratively pierced tin, to let in air and keep out flies.

Above left: The owners of this Duncan, South Carolina, farmhouse are collectors of old tables. Seen in a hallway is a sausage-grinding table with the grinder still attached. This table is used to display small arrangements. *Left:* This console table in front of a large living room window is actually a flour bin. The top lifts off to reveal the original tin-lined dividers for a variety of flours. *Above:* This detail photograph shows a corner of a living room in another nineteenth-century farmhouse.

Above: Utilitarian areas such as hallways and stair halls can also be used to display Americana. In this Victorian hallway, a mirrored walnut hat-hanger has been placed above a small marble-topped commode (useful for storage of boots and gloves). Ancestor photographs are displayed on a background of lively patterned Victorian wallpaper. *Right:* A spectacular effect has been achieved in this New Orleans hallway by the owners' use of a trompe l'oeil painting of a richly patterned rug on the wooden floor and stenciling on the storage wall doors. *Above right:* A stairwell wall is a perfect setting for a collection of nineteenth- and early-twentieth-century farm and carpentry tools.

Left: In a Connecticut bedroom, a glass-topped, fabric-skirted table is an attractive repository for books, ceramic houses, and a metal silhouette decoy. The quilt hung on the wall is attached with Velcro to a plywood and Velcro strip at the top of the quilt. *Below:* A tabletop in a Victorian bedroom accommodates a collection of old toys. *Below left:* Victorian door-stops, such as this ca. 1880 example, are highly sought-after collectibles.

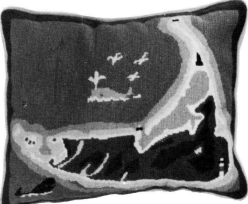

Above: The view from this Nantucket sitting room is so spectacular that its splendid collection of Victorian wicker could initially go unnoticed. *Right:* This needlepoint pillow has been crafted in a Nantucket map design. *Below:* The unifying element in this collection of antique perfume bottles is the Victorian look of the containers displayed before a triple mirror on a Victorian dresser.

Above right: The owners of this house are the son and daughter-in-law of Edward Deming and Faith Andrews, the pioneer scholars on the American Shakers, and they share an enthusiasm for the functional, clean-lined design of Shaker furniture. The rocking chair in the living room, made in 1801, is of the earliest Shaker type—the front legs join the rockers, which do not extend beyond. The red-painted bench beside the sofa is an example of those made by the Shakers in a variety of sizes and used in both dwellings and shops. This bench was found in a cellar of the Church family dwelling at the Hancock, Massachusetts, settlement. On top of the bench is a set of three boxes, a product for which the Shakers are well-known. To the right of the sofa is a three-legged candlestand that can be raised or lowered; it is original to the Church family at the Mount Lebanon, New York, community. The tin candlestick and extinguisher were made by the Shakers. Also at right is a wood box, which has retained its original red paint, with an open section on the bottom and shelf at the top. The portrait, painted in about 1840 by an unknown artist, depicts Garrett Volk of New York, an ancestor of one of the owners. *Above left:* This hickory slat-back armchair was made in the Mount Lebanon, New York, Shaker colony. *Below:* The simple lines and honest construction of these lapped oval boxes epitomize Shaker design. This graduated set was made in New England in the early nineteenth century, and the boxes have retained their original painted finishes.

Above left: The Shaker furniture in this part of the living room includes a rocking chair with a bar on top of the slats so that the piece could be upholstered if desired. Next to the rocking chair is a functional maple sewing stand with two sliding drawers, designed to enable two people to use the stand simultaneously. The pine chest of drawers, which retains its original red stain, came from the Hancock, Massachusetts, settlement, where it was made about 1830. At the left is an unpainted jelly cupboard with a faded blue oval box resting on its top. *Above:* This grain-painted pine cabinet/chest of drawers was made in the last half of the nineteenth century. *Left:* This pine chest of drawers has walnut drawer pulls and retains its original red paint. Inscribed on several of the drawers in pencil is "Sister's Office," where it was housed at the New Lebanon, New York, community in the middle of the nineteenth century.

Above: The wallpaper and the matching fabric in this window treatment in a Connecticut farmhouse are contemporary—Laura Ashley [R.G. #250]—but the bold "Meadow Flowers" pattern and elaborate swag-and-jabot valance treatment would be at home in a Victorian setting.

The room setting *above* contains a dresser and side chairs in the 1840s Gothic Revival style, but the wallpaper is a recent Brunschwig & Fils pattern, titled "Stonework," that simulates the look of Victorian castlelike houses [R.G. #233].

Auction house and dealer sales figures continue to show the great popularity of Shaker furniture and accessories among collectors. While there are now no Shaker communities making goods for sale, excellent reproductions, like the settee *below,* are being produced at the Shaker Workshops [R.G. #160], a company located in Concord, Massachusetts. The original of this handsome settee was crafted at the Mount Lebanon, New York, community shop.

Also seen frequently in Victorian homes were leather fire-buckets, *below,* which were filled with sand and kept near fireplaces. This handsomely painted pair, which bear the owner's name, "R. Durfee," and the date 1843, were auctioned for $650 at Skinner's auction house in 1983 [R.G. #85]. Fire-buckets are sometimes used today as wastebaskets, or umbrella stands.

Prosperous merchants and planters in the 1800s often commissioned artists to paint splendid portraits of themselves and their families. But the common man's portraiture was the silhouette—sometimes enhanced with a background sketch, as *above,* in the portrait of a hunter by Auguste T. Edouart, Savannah, Georgia, ca. 1840. This excellent example brought $800 at auction in 1982 (Christie's, New York [R.G. #74]).

Museum houses illustrated in this chapter that are open to the public (contact the museums for hours) are:

Melrose
1 Melrose-Montebello Parkway
Natchez, Mississippi 39120
601-445-4956 or 601-446-9408

Arlington
331 Cotton Avenue, S.W.
Birmingham, Alabama 35211
205-780-5656

The Brooklyn Museum
Eastern Parkway
Brooklyn, New York 11238
212-638-5000

Shakertown at Pleasant Hill, Kentucky
Route 4
Harrodsburg, Kentucky 40330
606-734-5411

Opposite: The furniture seen in this room and available at Shakertown in Pleasant Hill, Kentucky, is reproduced exactly from classically simple Shaker originals [R.G. #159].

Turn-of-the-Century Styles
1890–1914

Opposite: This house, built into a hill in Spring Green, Wisconsin, is Taliesin III, the home of the distinguished American architect Frank Lloyd Wright. Taliesin means "brow" in Welsh, and Wright wrote that his house should not be built *on* the hill but "should be *of* the hill, belonging to it, so that hill and house could live together each happier for the other." Originally built in 1902–1903, it burned twice and was finally rebuilt in 1925. *Above:* The dining room of an earlier Wright house (1895) in Oak Park, Illinois. To create a complete environment in many of his houses, Wright designed the furniture and lighting.

The last quarter of the nineteenth century, the Gilded Age, saw America's emergence as the world's greatest industrial power. Huge fortunes were amassed in railroading, the steel industry, oil, finance, and other pursuits. It was a time when great inventions—Thomas Edison's electric light and his phonograph, Alexander Graham Bell's telephone, George Eastman's mass-produced camera, and George Westinghouse's electric generator—seemed to make just about anything possible.

The 1900 census showed our population to be 76,994,575. Despite the steady growth of urban centers, the population remained essentially provincial, so the captains of industry called for, and got, legislation that raised immigration quotas. Millions came to America from all the nations of Europe and from Asia to work in the mills, mines, and factories, and on the railroads.

Adequate and commodious housing was not available to so large an immigrant population, and

147

Left: This living room in a Los Angeles home contains Mission Oak furniture crafted by the Craftsman Workshops of Gustav Stickley. Stickley, an extraordinary artist-entrepreneur, was the primary philosopher and shaper of the Arts and Crafts movement in America at the turn of the century. The design ethic of the movement was "form follows function," and the characteristics of its products were plain lines, matchless construction, top-quality materials, and flawless proportions. *Top:* This Stickley workshop oak armchair was designed by Harvey Ellis, who often utilized wooden inlays such as the floral designs on the vertical slat and front legs. *Above:* This oak library table was made by the Limbert Furniture Company of Grand Rapids, which started manufacturing Mission Oak in 1903.

149

Top: This ranch house near Fort Garland, Colorado, is the summer residence of a New York couple. The house was built between 1914 and 1916 and provides a perfect setting for a large collection of Arts and Crafts furniture made during the same period. The owners, who are from a family of collectors, began by gathering furniture and decorative accessories made at Elbert Hubbard's Roycroft Shops at East Aurora, New York. *Above:* The art-pottery vases and plate are the product of the New Orleans Art Pottery Company (which became an adjunct of Sophie Newcomb College of Tulane University); they were made around 1900. As with many designs in the Arts and Crafts period, nature inspired the predominant motifs—animal and flower forms.

In furniture design, too, there continued to be both revival movements and new, innovative directions. At the Philadelphia Centennial of 1876, one of the most popular exhibits was a period room—specifically, a Colonial American kitchen. Although hardly accurate historically (illustrations of the room show a romanticized view of early American life; the room is so overcrowded with utensils one is tempted to label it a culinary obstacle course), it spurred an interest in the objects of our past. While some people

Above left: The dining room and living room of the Colorado ranch house are part of the same vast space, dominated on each end by rugged fieldstone fireplaces. The dining table and chairs, made of oak (like almost all products of the Roycroft shops), are marked with the Roycroft emblem—an orb and a cross. The candlesticks, one pair of copper and the other brass, are also Roycroft products. The gun case is an unusual Roycroft piece; it was made to order for the journalist Caspar Whitney, whose name is emblazoned across the front. The pottery on the table and in the Renaissance Revival cupboard (not a Roycroft piece) was made for the Roycroft Inn, which Elbert Hubbard built in East Aurora in 1903. Left: A Roycroft oak library table. The bottom shelf has cut-out ends with double key-and-tenon construction that harks back to earlier cabinetmaking techniques. Above right: This thirty-day wall clock, ca. 1890, has a case made of mahogany, and glass painted black with gold trim. Made by Seth Thomas of Thomaston, Connecticut, the clock, in its clean-cut design, presaged the Stickley and Roycroft trend to simplicity. Above middle: This table lamp combines the master craftsmanship of three turn-of-the-century workshops. The etched silver-plated shade is from the Tiffany stock, the incandescent glass base is from the Steuben glassworks, and the overall design is Roycroft.

turned to collecting such objects, others manufactured reproductions of American furniture, hardware, lighting devices, and metalwares. Furniture pieces made between the 1660s and the early 1800s were used as models. The leading reproduction company of Colonial wares was that owned by Wallace Nutting, about whom *The Magazine Antiques* wrote: ''Over the special domain of literal copies of early American furniture, Wallace Nutting still reigns supreme.''

Left: In this vast central room two fanlighted doors open from each long wall. The leather-upholstered Morris chairs are marked with the Roycroft emblem. Most upholstered furniture made at the Roycroft shops employed leather, and the brass or copper tacks used to affix the leather to the chair or sofa frame are generally prominently shown, in keeping with the honesty of construction of Arts and Crafts furniture. The footstool, oak taboret, and round oak pedestal table are all Roycroft pieces and could be early examples. The matching rosewood console tables against the wall are English, ca. 1850. All of the vases in the room are products of the Roycroft copper shop. The whimsical bear smoking stand was made in Germany in the nineteenth century. *Above:* This side chair was made by Dard Hunter, the chief designer at the Roycroft shops. Its inviting inscription, ''Sit down & rest thy weary bones,'' is carved into the seat back. The leather upholstery and copper tacks are original. Typical of Arts and Crafts furniture are the simple lines, generous proportions, and visible methods of joining each element of the chair.

155

Above right: A bedroom at the Roycroft Inn at East Aurora, New York, the town in which Elbert Hubbard (seen in the portrait on the wall) founded the Roycroft shops. Hubbard published magazines, pamphlets, books, and manufactured furniture, ironwork, and pottery. Established in 1895, the Roycroft shops by 1907 employed close to 500 workers. Both the pottery and the Mission-style furniture seen here are from the Roycroft shops. *Above:* A Roycroft oak armchair, ca. 1906.

The Arts and Crafts movement, like so many styles that preceded it, was imported from England and had blossomed in the United States by the end of the nineteenth century. In both countries the movement grew as a reaction against the industrialization of the decorative arts and the resultant deterioration in quality and loss of individuality of objects through mass production. The founders of the movement in England—John Ruskin and William Morris—advocated fine handcraftsmanship, citing the beautiful illuminated manuscripts of the Middle Ages as examples. As in America, bookmaking was one of the main concerns and successful contributions of the movement, but all types of objects, from metalwares to textiles, were crafted on both sides of the Atlantic.

In America the Arts and Crafts movement took root in much the same way that it had in England. Small communities of craftsmen were established under one leader who often had no artistic experience but who could foster their communal purpose or be the brains behind the business. Among these communities in America, the Craftsman Workshops of Gustav Stickley were most

Above left: In the library of the Colorado house (seen on the preceding pages) are a Roycroft oak slant-front desk, ca. 1906, a Roycroft wastebasket, and a copper vase made in the Roycroft copper shop. The horn chair pulled up to the desk is Austrian. The Remington drawing and the painting—*North American Buffalo*—are particularly well suited to this western house. *Above:* This hall coat-and-hat rack, fashioned in part with steer horns, was made in Texas at the turn of the century.

notable. His furniture was praised by one contemporary as "entitled to the distinction of [being] the one distinctly American School of Design." As seen in examples pictured on pages 148–151, Stickley's Mission Oak furniture was characterized by severely plain lines, flawless proportions, and top-quality wood, finish, and workmanship.

Stickley's principal competitor in the marketplace was Elbert Hubbard, whose Roycroft Shops community in East Aurora, New York, produced impressive quantities of furniture, pottery, leather, and metal objects.

Other notable centers producing pottery in this style, which is simply called "art pottery," were Newcomb College in New Orleans *(see page 152)* and Rookwood Pottery in Cincinnati.

Many in the Arts and Crafts movement also worked in the international style termed Art Nouveau, which was largely based on curvilinear, sensuously flowing lines and intricate ornamentation. Although the dominance of this style was relatively brief, the influence of its major proponents has been considerable.

Foremost among the many American Art Nouveau craftsmen was Louis Comfort Tiffany, who created extraordinarily beautiful stained-glass windows, lamps, glass, and ceramics *(see pages 172–175).*

Finally, one of the interesting side currents in American design was the popularity of rustic furniture—chairs, tables, and other furniture made from bent saplings, as well as pieces made from animal horn *(see pages 157–163).* These romantic oddities fit right in with the love of the outdoors championed by the energetic Teddy Roosevelt, our president in 1901.

Top: This romantic bedroom, with leaded- and stained-glass windows characteristic of the turn of the century, contains wicker, a painted metal bed, and lots of flowers. *Right:* The use of flora and fauna as design elements was a hallmark of the Arts and Crafts movement. This carved and painted walnut wall cabinet is a prime example. The piece is topped with carved sunflowers that also separate the two sections of the cabinet, which are decorated with landscape panels. *Above:* This sterling-silver inkstand was sold by the shop of John Wanamaker in 1900. The silver crab is on a porcelain base painted to simulate a beach.

Left: Art Nouveau furniture of the high quality of workmanship of this lady's desk is very rare. The desk is made primarily of mahogany and mahogany veneers. It stands on lyre-shaped supports at each end and is richly carved with acanthus leaves and tulips. The Brooklyn Museum, its owner, dates the piece ca. 1900. *Above:* This architectural panel from a Short Hills, New Jersey, mansion, ca. 1900, was designed by William W. Renwick.

159

Below: This New England country cabin is a perfect showcase for the currently popular rustic decorating look. *Below right:* A bison head and an Indian child hunter decorate this unusual bronze door knocker, ca. 1900–1910. *Right:* A group of metal doorstops of the same period: large and small rabbits, a frog, and a proud eagle.

160

Below: This interior view of the cabin epitomizes the cozy, rustic decorating style. A decoy, a sporting painting, and a collection of metal and ceramic hunting dogs on the beam mantel all contribute to the ambiance. *Left:* From the late nineteenth century, this hooked rug features a prancing horse.

Top: This turn-of-the-century photograph shows a hunting lodge near Lake Placid in the Adirondack Mountains in upstate New York—filled with rustic "twig" furniture. This distinctive furniture was fashioned from saplings of the local forest by native guides during the off-season. *Above:* This mallard duck decoy was made in the early twentieth century by the Mason Decoy Factory in Detroit, Michigan. *Right:* A wooden "stick up" mourning dove decoy carved in New England early in this century.

162

Above: A rustic *tête-à-tête* settee, made by contemporary furniture maker Gilbert Jaques. *Right:* This twig cradle was made in New York about 1890. It has arched ends, and the elaborate bent-twig construction is fashioned into hearts, hoops, and circles. *Above right:* A primitive candle-stand, with five tree-branch legs, made in New England ca. 1890.

163

Above: An old photograph of a rustic porch overlooking Lake Placid. The porch railing is fashioned from saplings, and the furniture is a mix of wicker and country pieces. *Right:* Two lolling chairs of the style termed simply "Adirondack chair."

Left: This collection of antique and contemporary American blankets and coverlets is artfully displayed on a stairway wall and railing. *Below:* A turn-of-the-century Navajo saddle blanket. *Bottom:* A remarkable collection of Tennessee crafts is displayed in the living room of the Director of Visual Arts, Crafts, and Folk Arts of the Tennessee Arts Commission. Hanging in the window are berry baskets, each formed from a single piece of bark curved to fit against the leg of a kneeling berry picker. The split-oak baskets lined up on the top shelf were made in the mountains of east Tennessee.

165

Above right: At the turn of the century, Grand Rapids furniture, and the products of other furniture manufacturing centers, tended to be styled in the current fashions—or to follow after a few years such new developments as the Stickley and Roycroft Mission style. This comfortable living room features a suite of golden-oak furniture adapted from the Mission style. *Above:* A handsome Arts and Crafts style oak tall clock made by the New Haven Clock Company, ca. 1915. *Right:* A cut-glass punch bowl, and glass and silver-plate ladle, ca. 1910.

Above left: This dining room grouping consists of a golden-oak pedestal table with carved lion-paw feet, and oak chairs with designs steam-pressed on their backs. Steam pressing was a mass-production decorative technique that would have been eschewed by Stickley or the Roycroft workshops. *Above:* A golden-oak side chair, also of early-twentieth-century manufacture. *Left:* A large India rug with a Grecian-key border design imported by Gustav Stickley, ca. 1910.

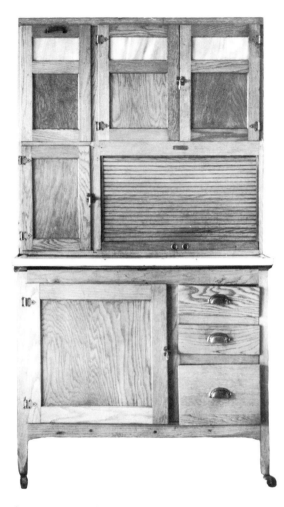

Above right: A working early-twentieth-century gas stove is a cherished showpiece in this farmhouse kitchen, which is enhanced by a collection of hanging baskets delineating a hallway. *Above and right:* Golden-oak kitchen cabinetry is highly collectible today. The icebox *right* was manufactured in Buffalo, New York, ca. 1910. The Hoosier-type cabinet *above* is of the same era; it contains a built-in flour bin and sifter.

Opposite page; top right: An unusual collection of early-twentieth-century rug beaters and various carpenter's tools is displayed on this kitchen wall. *Top left:* Another specialized collection displayed on a kitchen wall—in this case a grouping of eight vintage food choppers. *Below left:* This attractive living-room Christmas display was achieved by hanging an evergreen swag above a collection of old candlesticks and other collectibles on the mantel. *Below right:* Another mantel display uses an old advertisement for beef as its centerpiece.

Below: The oak rolltop desk is certainly one of the most sought-after forms of late-Victorian or turn-of-the-century furniture. The style was mass-produced by Grand Rapids, North Carolina, and other manufacturing centers from the 1870s on. *Left:* An Arts and Crafts style oak and wrought-iron table lamp, ca. 1910, attributed to Gustav Stickley. *Below left:* The Regulator wall clock was a standard fixture in schools, railroad stations, and offices across America. This model was manufactured in Connecticut in 1906. *Opposite:* This bedroom demonstrates the exuberant late-Victorian early-twentieth-century decorating style that seemed to dictate ''more is better''. . . more patterns, colors, and shapes. The mix of two quilts and patterned wallpaper does not create a tranquil room, but it definitely evokes the style of the time. The oak bed is ca. 1890.

Above: Built in 1977–1982 by architect Don M. Ramos, this Beverly Hills, California, house is stylistically one of the most unusual to be built in the United States in many years. It is designed in the mode of the Art Nouveau architecture practiced at the turn of the century in the Midwest by Louis Sullivan, in Spain by Antonio Gaudí, and in France by Hector Guimard. Built for a dealer in Art Nouveau and Art Deco art and antiques, the house represents the best in twentieth-century reproduction craftsmanship. *Above right:* Each corner of the house's recreation room has a beautifully crafted plaster sculpture of one of the four seasons. This one is Summer, by designer Joe Ishikawa. The bronze, by Vallnais, is early twentieth century. *Top:* A contemporary reproduction by David Woolsey of Louis Comfort Tiffany's classic Wisteria lamp. *Right:* An Art Nouveau laminated mahogany and maple armchair with carved Egyptian lotus blossoms, American, ca. 1910.

Above left: The recreation room of the Beverly Hills house contains an extraordinary collection of Art Nouveau furniture and lighting. The great French designers of the period—who were in fashion during the Belle Epoch in America as well—are represented here in lighting fixtures by Galle and Lalique. The elaborately painted and plaster-sculpted ceiling was designed by Nick Heflinger. *Above:* Bats are the principal design motif in this exotic room—in both the plaster sculpture and the stained-glass window by Mayra Art Glass Studio. *Left:* This laminated mahogany armchair is from Boston, ca. 1920. Its intricate carvings of intertwining scrolls on the back, with leaf and shell carvings running into the arms and down the legs, are typical motifs of the Art Nouveau movement.

Above: A high-ceilinged loft office in New York serves as a gallery for a collection of nineteenth- and early twentieth-century American graphics. The collector, a Southerner, has hung a grouping of Confederate militaria above a ca. 1880 pine mantelpiece salvaged in Mobile: three 1903 chromoliths of Confederate soldiers by William L. Sheppard, an 1850 Alabama map, and a Kurz and Allison Civil War battle print in a shadow box with lead Confederate soldiers. The fire screen below the mantel is a painted sign of the Alabama state seal from a late-nineteenth-century industrial exhibit held in New Orleans. On the wall at right is a grouping of war posters from the Spanish-American, First and Second World wars. *Right:* An adjustable brass student lamp with a green glass shade—an early electric fixture, ca. 1895.

Finishing Touches

Furniture like the Mission-style side chair, ca. 1910, *below,* from the workshop of L. and J.G. Stickley, is gaining in popularity. This chair was part of a set sold at the Skinner auction house. Similar chairs can still be found for under $200 [R.G. #85].

At the turn of the century, American artists of genius were coming into prominence in many media—architecture, fine art, and the decorative arts. The studio of Louis Comfort Tiffany, which designed magnificent metalwork and glasswork, created the original of the reproduction stained-glass window *above.* Titled *View of Oyster Bay,* the reproduction is 13¼ by 12¼ inches; it is available from the Metropolitan Museum of Art [R.G. #220]. Mary Cassatt was a young Philadelphian who studied in Paris and was greatly influenced by the Impressionists. Cassatt's *La Toilette,* reproduced in the poster *below* from the Boston Museum of Fine Arts [R.G. #210], was painted in 1891.

Home crafts were a major element in the Arts and Crafts movement in the early part of this century. An anonymous master of needlework made the intricate, eight-panel needlepoint rug or wall hanging, *above,* depicting the story of Snow White. This piece was auctioned by Phillips, New York [R.G. #83].

Shades of the Past, of Corte Madera, California [R.G. #203], is a company that re-creates ornate turn-of-the-century silk lampshades and brass bases. "The Tiffany," *below,* has a shade with a leaded glass fleur-de-lis center, velvet top and bottom, antique gold trim, and Venetian-glass bead fringe.

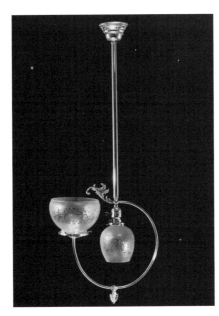

The graceful chandelier *above* is a faithful reproduction of a brass combination electric and gas model manufactured around 1890. It is available from The Classic Illumination of Oakland, California [R.G. #191].

Prices of antique duck and shorebird decoys have soared. Some of the most desirable antique decoys were made at the Mason Decoy Factory in Detroit early in this century. Now, Will Kirkpatrick, a master carver, has founded Shorebird Decoys, Inc., of Hudson, Massachusetts [R.G. #219], and produces a wide range of reproductions, including the Mason *above*.

The trotting horse hooked rug *above* is a contemporary craft product of The Agèd Ram of Essex Junction, Vermont [R.G. #91]. Suzanne and Cleland Selbey, who create the colorful rugs, sometimes reproduce antique rugs but also create new designs based on folk art symbols—weather vanes, quilt patterns, toys, and others.

Old country-made game boards are, like many collectibles, both decorative and utilitarian. This attractive hand-painted pine checkerboard is new. It is available from the Winterthur Reproductions Catalog [R.G. #230].

The Amish courting seat *above* is a product of the Amish Country Store [R.G. #114] of New Castle, Pennsylvania. The settee-rocker, of oak and hickory bent-twig construction, is also available in cherry or walnut with hickory.

Above: Around 1900 master metalsmith Robert J. Jarvie fashioned the original of this striking pair of Arts and Crafts candlesticks, a Metropolitan Museum of Art reproduction [R.G. #220].

Lenox, a leading porcelain manufacturer today, produced this Art Nouveau Belleek humidor early in this century. It was sold at Boston's Robert W. Skinner auction house [R.G. #85] for $150.

The original of the fabric *above* was designed in 1891 by William Morris, one of the founders of the Arts and Crafts movement in England. This pattern, "Daffodil," is from a line of Morris reproduction fabrics available from Scalamandré Silks [R.G. #108].

Museum houses illustrated in this chapter that are open to the public (contact the museums for hours) are:

"Hillside" of the Taliesin Fellowship
WIS 23
Spring Green, Wisconsin
608-588-2511

Frank Lloyd Wright Home and Studio
951 Chicago Avenue at Forest Avenue
Oak Park, Illinois 60302
312-848-1978

Opposite: The turn-of-the-century rustic, or Adirondack, look has become so popular again that such leading designers as Ralph Lauren are creating linens in complementary styles. This rustic bed is dressed in Lauren's North Woods line [R.G. #260].

Eclectic Twentieth-Century Styles 1915–1984

Opposite: Atlanta architect Norman Davenport Askins designed this traditional cedar-shingled house in Highlands, North Carolina, in close consultation with its owners, who wanted a comfortable, modern weekend-retreat that would be an appropriate setting for their collection of American nineteenth-century antiques and contemporary crafts. *Above:* The free association of styles of very different periods is increasingly popular in the late twentieth century. This dining room combines turn-of-the-century oak with sleek Breuer chairs designed in 1928.

During the first years of World War I, which erupted in Europe in 1914, President Woodrow Wilson called on the American people to support his policy of neutrality. But in 1917, when German submarines sank several U.S. ships, with a loss of hundreds of American lives, the United States joined England and France in the final campaigns that spelled defeat for Germany the following year.

America was proud of General Pershing and the "doughboys" and of their contribution to the Allied victory. The great wave of patriotism that swept the country in the postwar period did much to maintain the popular taste for furniture in the early-American style. Mass production of such pieces continued in Grand Rapids and in other furniture centers.

In the 1920s America was an international leader in the field of architecture, with innovators like Frank Lloyd Wright, Bernard Maybeck, and Raymond Hood in the forefront. Technological advances had

Opposite: The living room of the Highlands house is a warm mix of antique furnishings and comfortable upholstered seating furniture, slip-covered in summer in washable sailcloth. The cherry desk is a family piece from Kentucky. The saber-legged chairs are Federal-style. The Windsor chairs are reproductions crafted in Connecticut. Above an antique pine mantel found in Pennsylvania is an elephant folio Audubon print, *Eider Ducks.* A collection of Staffordshire plates and figures is displayed in the bookcases. The green, six-board blanket box, from Union County, North Carolina, has "made in one day" inscribed on the inside of the lid. *Above left:* Seen above the sofa in another view of the living room is an important early-French map, *Henry Moozon's North and South Carolina,* ca. 1777. (Highlands was in the uncharted wilderness.) The Oriental rug is a Heriz. The pillows and sofa are covered in salvaged pieces of antique overshot coverlets. *Above right:* Adjoining the living room, master bedroom, and dining room is a screened gallery with a panoramic view of the Appalachians. It is furnished with contemporary rockers made in North Carolina, Mexican side chairs, and an antique country settee. Seen through the door is the dining area, where a Pennsylvania corner cupboard, ca. 1820, houses a collection of blue-and-white Staffordshire.

Several important artistic trends influenced Art Deco's stylistic evolution. One was the rise of cubism, especially in the work of such artists as Pablo Picasso and Georges Braque. Another influence was the work of the Vienna Werkstatte, whose leading architect-designer, Josef Hoffmann, has been unofficially credited with founding the modern movement in Europe. The design motifs of North and Central American Indians—particularly of the Aztec and Navajo cultures—as well as primitive sculpture of northern Africa also provided inspiration for the modernist designers.

The Art Deco movement sought to simplify the lines of furnishings for reasons of esthetics and to adapt design to the conditions of mass production. Two of the foremost furniture designers in the Art Deco style in America were Eliel Saarinen, an architect *(see pages 189, 197, 198)*, and Paul Theodore Frankl, who, in his 1928 book *New Dimensions,* wrote, "Meaningless ornaments should be avoided as much as possible. Restraint is a very important factor in modern design."

If restraint is at the core of Art Deco, minimalism is foremost in the International style, which has been a dominant factor in America from 1930 up to the present.

The style has its roots in the Bauhaus, a highly influential school founded in Germany in 1919. Its founder, Walter Gropius, believed that for this century, art and technology must be intimately linked. Bauhaus students were taught by two instructors—an artist and a craftsman. Among the notable Bauhaus graduates who came to America was Ludwig Mies van der Rohe, whose less-is-more architecture and furniture *(see page 187)* have won the highest critical praise. Eero Saarinen, the son of Eliel Saarinen, was another master of the International style. He, like Mies van der Rohe, was both an architect and a designer of furniture *(see pages 198–199)*.

As the twentieth century proceeded—through the Depression of the 1930s, World War II, and the ensuing decades—American taste became more and more eclectic.

While variations on International purism (such as the high-tech use of industrial materials in home furnishings) have come and gone, several styles seem to have become almost classic in their own right. The elegant minimalism of the International style is one. Another style that has endured is the country look—the use of American country furnishings and folk art, both in country houses and city apartments and lofts. In the end, as Alexandra Stoddard pointed out in her essay on decorating in the present day, *the American Classic style is a highly personal mixture of fine pieces in forms both traditional and modern.*

made possible what was to become the all-American architectural form—the skyscraper. In 1922 Hood's firm won a competition held for the design of a skyscraper headquarters for the *Chicago Tribune.* Entries had been submitted by 260 architects from around the world.

In the decorative arts, however, until the 1930s American designers were in a stagnant period. In 1924, in fact, Secretary of Commerce Herbert Hoover regretfully declined to enter American wares in the important Paris Exposition des Arts Décoratifs et Industriels Modernes. It was required that objects displayed be both original and modern, and Mr. Hoover could not muster a diverse group of American objects that met those criteria.

It was at this landmark exposition that the Art Moderne, or Art Deco, style was launched. One critic has termed Art Deco "the last of the great truly cohesive decorative arts styles." Furniture in this style was often chrome-plated, tubular, enameled, and leather-upholstered. Instead of the sinuous curves of Art Nouveau, Art Deco employed hard-edged geometric designs such as zigzags, lightning bolts, sun rays, and streamlined representations of human and animal forms.

Opposite: This warm, hospitable kitchen is a perfect forum for the culinary enterprises of the owner of the Highlands house, who has become, since his retirement, a gourmet weekend cook. On the work island rests an attractive centerpiece arrangement—an old tool box filled with fresh vegetables. The exposed old pine beams, featured throughout the house, were salvaged from an Augusta, Georgia, warehouse. *Left:* The kitchen fireplace wall is painted with red stain, here decorated with native flowers. The small rockers are late-nineteenth-century family pieces; the settee and wing chair are reproductions. *Above:* A north-facing bedroom in the Highlands house is made inviting and cozy by a deep red wall paint ("Scarlett O'Hara" red) and a corner fireplace, here filled with country flowers that include green "dog hobble," a native plant. The pine pencil-post beds were made by Jack Campbell, an Athens, Tennessee, craftsman. The Kilim rug picks up the red, green, navy, and cream colors of the early-nineteenth-century Jacquard overshot coverlets. *Above left:* Seen near the bedroom fireplace is a comfortable reproduction wing chair and a child's toy chest that serves as a side table. The comb-back Windsor rocker is nineteenth-century, as are the print and the English Staffordshire figure above the mantel.

Marcel Breuer, a student and later master of the furniture workshop at the Bauhaus—an immensely influential school of art and design in Germany (1919–1933)—was the designer of all three of these classic International-style tubular steel pieces. Breuer's inspiration for this furniture, with its simple lines and great strength, was, it is said, the handlebars of his bicycle. *Above:* A rare Breuer glass and chromium plated tubular steel cocktail table ca. 1928 from the collection of the Brooklyn Museum. *Above left:* This sleek armchair of canvas and leather with a chrome-plated steel tube frame was designed by Breuer ca. 1925. *Left:* This classic Breuer side chair—called the Cesca chair—is his most famous design. First manufactured in 1928, it has been imitated in many variations throughout the world. *Opposite:* This town house dining area illustrates the "less is more" emphasis of the International style (ca. 1930–1980)—an emphasis on unadorned architectural details and simple, functional furnishings, often architect designed. Seen here are Eero Saarinen's molded plastic pedestal table and Marcel Breuer's Cesca side chairs of polished chrome tubular steel.

Opposite: The living room shown here is in the New Canaan, Connecticut, home of the distinguished American architect Philip Johnson. Called simply "the glass house," it is one of the most famous residences designed in this century. For his furniture, Johnson selected the work of master Bauhaus architect Ludwig Mies van der Rohe, who had designed the stainless steel and leather Barcelona chair (it was introduced at an exposition in that city) in 1929. Many critics regard this combination of classic Roman form and materials produced with modern technology as the most influential chair design of the twentieth century. *Top:* Johnson's classic glass house, designed in 1949. *Right:* The Barcelona table of stainless steel and glass and the simple leather-covered couch on a stainless steel frame, *above,* were also designed by Mies van der Rohe.

While the term "Grand Rapids furniture" has sometimes been used to connote cheap reproductions, Michigan has been, in fact, one of the leading innovative design centers for much of this century. Since the early 1930s, the Herman Miller furniture company in Zeeland, Michigan, has been manufacturing the original designs of top architects and industrial designers. Miller's first chief designer was Gilbert Rohde, whose use of Art Deco forms and modern technology is evident in this upholstered living room furniture, *above.* The Art Deco gilt metal and glass table lamp, *left,* was made in the early 1920s.

The Cranbrook Academy of Art/Museum in Bloomfield Hills, Michigan, is a repository for many examples of the best American-designed furniture and lighting of the Art Deco period. The dining room, *above right,* in the president's house at Cranbrook is filled with the designs of Eliel Saarinen, a distinguished architect and the institution's president in the early 1930s. The table and chairs are made of fir, ebony, hare, holly, and boxwood. The aluminum floor lamp, *above,* made by the Nessen Company, is also a Saarinen design. *Right:* Saarinen designed this simple but stylish buffet, with geometric inlays of walnut, ebony, and maple veneers, in 1930.

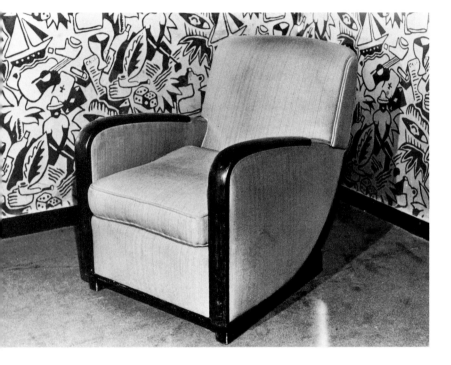

Many critics and historians have written that the skyscraper at its best—as in New York's Rockefeller Center, a rich blending of functional planning, high technology, and esthetics—is America's greatest architectural achievement. The thirty-one-story building at 50th Street and the Avenue of the Americas, shown *above right,* houses at its base the world's largest indoor theater, Radio City Music Hall. Rockefeller Center today comprises nineteen buildings on nearly 21 acres. Its first building was opened in 1932. *Above:* The interior design and much of the furnishings for Radio City Music Hall were created by Donald Deskey, a leading designer in the 1930s. This chair is seen in the second mezzanine men's lounge in the Music Hall. Deskey's wall mural, titled ''Nicotine,'' depicts the production of tobacco from field to finished product. It is painted on aluminum foil provided by the American Tobacco Company. *Right:* A small Deskey table in the simple Bauhaus tradition in modern design. Its top is black lacquered wood and the three-part base is aluminum.

Seen *above* in Radio City Music Hall is the studio apartment of its first director, S.L. "Roxy" Rothafel, which is tucked away in an upper floor of the theater. The interior of the apartment is a tour de force of Donald Deskey's design abilities, with his tables, chairs, and lighting coordinated to a simple formal theme. This view is from the living room looking into the dining room. *Below left:* This twin-pedestal Art Deco style Deskey cabinet is black lacquered wood with two glass shelves and has built-in lighting. *Below:* A wrought-iron and molded-glass Art Deco table lamp, ca. 1930.

Opposite: This library in the Art Deco style is at the Brooklyn Museum. Seating furniture in this style tended to be chunky and curvaceous, as in the wicker chair, ca. 1937, *top,* seen on a Connecticut porch; the chair is beneath a 1935 Nantucket poster by Tony Sarg. *Above:* A bamboo porch-armchair imported from Manila, the Philippines, in 1930. Since their introduction to America in the mid-nineteenth century, wicker and rattan have been fashioned into furniture in each succeeding style period.

Both pieces shown here, the desk by Gilbert Rohde, ca. 1941, *above,* and the coffee table *opposite bottom,* by Isamu Noguchi, ca. 1947, reflect a growing movement in the 1940s toward a sculptured component in American furniture design. Rohde's double-pedestal kidney-shaped desk is made of paldao wood. The pedestal sides are covered in leather cloth with antique brass studs. The desk and the coffee table are products of the Herman Miller Company. Miller's chief designer, George Nelson, commissioned a number of top designers to find fresh ways to bring together in mass-produced furniture both good design and creative incorporation of technological advances. Noguchi's glass-and-walnut table, free-flowing and abstract, is much akin to his sculpture.

Museum exhibitions and competitions have always exerted great influence on trends in interior design, and the 1941 Museum of Modern Art International Design Competition was no exception. Perhaps the competition's impact was most dramatic in the category of seating furniture. Two of the winners—Charles Eames and Eero Saarinen, then young architects at Cranbrook Academy—went on to become major figures in twentieth-century design. Their chairs and sofas, made of such materials as bent plywood, foam rubber, and other plastics used in new ways,

were curved to fit the human body. *Above:* In 1946, Eames and his wife/collaborator, Ray, designed this plywood dining chair—"the potato chip chair"—which is still listed in Miller's catalog. *Above left:* This form-fitting shell-constructed upholstered chair was designed by Eero Saarinen in 1948 for New York's Knoll Associates. Called the womb chair, it was described by Saarinen as "a great big chair you can curl up in."

Few decades in the history of American decorative arts have rivaled the 1950s for design productivity. The room *opposite* contains a suite of Eero Saarinen's simple and graceful molded plastic and metal pedestal furniture. Beginning in 1933, Saarinen built scale model prototypes of this design to try out on his family. His goal, he stated, was to clear up "the slum of legs" beneath chairs and tables. Knoll Associates introduced this Saarinen line in 1956. *Below:* Also introduced in 1956—by Herman Miller—is this now classic lounge chair and ottoman. It is Charles Eames's most celebrated design, a perfect synthesis of technology and materials—here rosewood veneer, molded plywood, cast aluminum, and upholstery—with comfort and esthetics. *Right:* Sculptor and designer Harry Bertoia, like Saarinen and Eames a Cranbrook Academy alumnus, designed this "chickenwire chair" for Knoll Associates in 1950.

199

Under the design leadership of Gilbert Rohde in the 1930s and early 1940s and of architect George Nelson thereafter, Herman Miller has been an innovator in both office and residential furniture design. *Above:* Designed in 1956, this modular seating system is easily adapted to many spaces and uses. *Opposite page:* This 1967 seating group, called the Cube Group, shows Nelson's expertise in combining integrity of design with technological innovations. *Top:* This unique 1956 Nelson design is called the Marshmallow Love Seat. One critic commented that "striking as it is, even marshmallows would have a difficult courtship."

This cedar-shingled barn, *top left,* in northwestern Connecticut has been creatively converted into a weekend house by a New York family, who wanted a cozy house but also wanted to retain the barn's "personality." The staircase, *right,* is constructed of two twenty-four-foot, solid oak beams. The fitted-pipe railings and hanging factory lights are of a decorating style that came to be called, in the 1970s, high tech. In the forty-two-foot-high stairwell hang a Virginia-made quilt and an ancestor portrait, ca. 1840. Above the fireplace in the comfortable living room, *top right,* is seen the matching portrait of a great-great-great-grandparent. *Above:* The kitchen walls are the unstained pine boards of the two cattle stalls originally in this space. The floor tile is Mexican and radiant-heated; with a southern exposure, the winter sun alone can raise the temperature in the room into the 80s. The bentwood chairs are of a design by the French architect Le Corbusier.

This striking Connecticut house, *top*, constructed of stone, wood, and glass, was designed by architect John Johanson. The interior design is twentieth-century eclectic at its best. *Left:* Several levels are connected by open staircases with metal railings. The air conditioning and heating ducts are left exposed. At the top of one landing is a magnificent English Chippendale secretary-bookcase, lacquered and decorated by English craftsmen who had traveled to China to master that demanding skill. *Above:* The sideboard and dining room table, both English of the eighteenth century, seem right at home with the classic Breuer Cesca side chairs designed almost two hundred years later.

Historically, American architects have designed furniture and other decorative furnishings as well as buildings. Jefferson designed furniture for Monticello; Frank Lloyd Wright liked to design all the interior elements for his houses—the furniture, lighting, and even decorative windows. Architects today are no exception. The black lacquer conference/dining table and chair *above and left,* inspired by a 1906 Austrian design, are by Richard Meier. *Below:* This dining room table by Connecticut cabinetmaker Ed Lucca is custom-made of Honduras mahogany, curly maple, ebony, and primavera.

The most dramatic trend in architectural and interior design in America in the 1980s is the rejection by a number of architects and industrial designers of the "less is more" tenet of the Bauhaus and of International-style modernism. Michael Graves, the architect of the "Post-Modern" house in Warren, New Jersey, *above,* is—like many twentieth-century architects—a designer as well. A leading, if controversial, proponent of Post-Modernism, Graves is fascinated by the challenge of developing new ways to incorporate classical design elements into contemporary architecture and furnishings. *Right:* An upholstered bird's-eye

maple lounge chair of Graves's design. The showroom *left* was designed by Graves and contains upholstered furniture designed by Lella and Massimo Vignelli. The geometric wooden cocktail table by Gianfranco Frattini is called a kioto table; it was inspired by a classic Japanese wood-working technique.

205

Finishing Touches

The sophisticated lady in the cloche who graces the poster *above* exemplifies the Art Deco look of the 1930s. Titled *Deco Lady*, it is produced by the Art Poster Company of Southfield, Minnesota [R.G. #207].

The revival of the 1930s Art Deco decorating style in the 1970s and 1980s has prompted the linens and accessories industry to introduce new lines with the Deco look. The bed *below* is dressed in an elegant pattern, called "Luxury Liner," by J.P. Stevens [R.G. #265]. The ensemble includes a comforter, tailored bedskirt, pillow slips, and sheets.

Merriam-Webster defines "classic" as "of the highest quality or rank—having recognized and permanent value." Americans are fortunate in having had architects and designers working here in this century who have created buildings and furniture that are already recognized as classic. Several architects have designed both buildings and furniture of this quality: Mies van der Rohe with his Seagram Building, his 1929 Barcelona chair, and Barcelona table, *above*, for example; Eero Saarinen and his CBS Building and pedestal furniture also clearly qualify. This furniture, as well as Charles Eames's classic 1956 lounge chair and ottoman, *below*, is—happily—still being produced. Knoll International [R.G. #147] manufactures the Mies line, and Herman Miller Inc. [R.G. #151] is the source for the Saarinen and Eames collections.

The handsome etched-glass chandelier *above* is a precise copy by The Classic Illumination of Oakland, California [R.G. #191], of a 1920s original. The base is polished brass.

Marcel Breuer, the designer of the chair *below*, was, like Mies van der Rohe, an alumnus of the famous Bauhaus design school. This "Wassily" chair of polished tubular steel and canvas was the first chair to be built of bent tubular steel—a major design innovation. Designed in 1925, the Wassily chair is still available from Knoll International [R.G. #147].

This 1930s table lamp is called "Silhouette Nymph." The disc shade she holds is frosted glass and the base is metal with a high-gloss black enamel finish. The lamp is a product of Sarsaparilla Deco Designs Limited of West New York, New Jersey [R.G. #226].

Brunschwig & Fils [R.G. #233] is the source of the sophisticated wallpaper pattern, "Art Greco," *above*. It is well suited to one of the current decorating trends that utilizes "Post-Modern" classical motifs in simple—but not "stripped down"—modern approaches.

The seating system *below* is called "Sistema 61" and is from Castelli Furniture, of Bohemia, New York [R.G. #122]. It consists of cubes of injection-molded foam rubber and polyurethane frames that may be arranged in an endless number of configurations.

In the 1950s Frank Lloyd Wright, one of America's greatest architects, tried with limited success to create a line of mass-market fabrics for F. Schumacher [R.G. #109]. *Below:* A handsome linen print from that now discontinued "Taliesin" line.

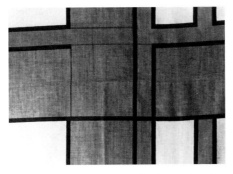

This extension desk lamp is the design of Robert Sonneman, an award-winning industrial designer of lighting. It is available in either chrome or solid brass from George Kovacs Lighting [R.G. #194].

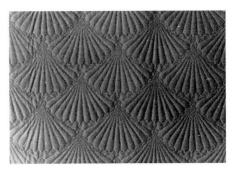

This cotton fabric in a sophisticated shell-like pattern called "Coquillage Metalasse" is available in six colors from Brunschwig & Fils [R.G. #233].

Widely utilized by Post-Modern aficionados, this elegant column is an "up light" from the pioneering firm of George Kovacs Lighting, of New York [R.G. #194]. It stands 73 inches high and is 14 inches in diameter.

Museum houses illustrated in this chapter that are open to the public (contact the museums for hours) are:

Cranbrook Academy of Art
500 Lone Pine Road
Bloomfield, Michigan
313-645-3000

The Brooklyn Museum
Eastern Parkway
Brooklyn, New York 11238
212-638-5000

Resource Guide

The Resource Guide to DECORATING WITH AMERICANA provides listings of reputable sources for antiques (dealers and auction houses), period reproductions, materials, and accessories. As far as possible, the specialties of the sources listed have been identified by period and type of merchandise offered. The codes used are as follows: C = Colonial, F = Federal, AE = American Empire, V = Victorian, T = Turn-of-the-century, Cy = Contemporary, MO = Mail Order, LA = Literature Available, RO = Retail Outlets, DLA = Dealer List Available, TO = Trade Only (through decorators).

Resource Guide photo credits: see Acknowledgements.

Antique Dealers

1. America Hurrah
766 Madison Avenue
New York, NY 10021
212-535-1930
Nineteenth-century quilts and American folk art

2. Antiquarian Traders
8483 Melrose Avenue
Los Angeles, CA 90069
213-658-6394
Leases and sells antique furniture in a variety of nineteenth-century styles

3. Graham Arader
1000 Boxwood Court
King of Prussia, PA 19406
215-825-6570
Prints

4. Balene, Inc.
2005 West Gray
Houston, TX 77019
713-523-2304
American Indian, African, and pre-Columbian art

5. Joan Bogart
P.O. Box 265
Rockville Centre, NY 11571
516-764-0529
Decorative arts of the nineteenth century
Gallery: 617 Seaman Avenue, Baldwin, NY

6. Pam Boynton
Pleasant Street
Groton, MA 01450
617-448-5031
Eighteenth-century New England country furniture and accessories

7. Philip H. Bradley Company
East Lancaster Avenue (Route 30)
Downingtown, PA 19335
215-269-0427, 215-269-8173
Eighteenth- and early-nineteenth-century American furniture

8. J. Camp Gallery
380 West Broadway
New York, NY 10012
212-966-3372
North American tribal art

9. Coe-Kerr Gallery
49 East 82nd Street
New York, NY 10028
212-628-1340
Nineteenth- and twentieth-century American art

10. Lillian Cogan
22 High Street
Farmington, CT 06032
203-677-9259
Pilgrim Century furniture and accessories

11. Country Store
28 James Street
Geneva, IL 60134
C, V, T, Cy
Country decorative accessories, handwoven and braided rugs, kitchen antiques, Hoosiers, and pine furniture
MO, LA at $2

12. Corey Daniels Antiques
RFD 2, Box 377
Wells, ME 04090
207-646-5301
C, F
Early country and formal furniture, accessories, decorative arts, and folk art
RO

13. David Dunton
RFD 1
Woodbury, CT 06798
203-263-5355
American-made furniture of the early years of the Republic and Federal-period paintings and accessories

14. Echo Antiques
415 Third Avenue
New York, NY 10016
212-689-4241
V, T, Cy
Antiques, furniture, lighting, and accessories of the Art Deco period

15. The Exhumation: Nick Procaccino
P.O. Box 2057
Princeton, NJ 08540
609-921-2339
Turn-of-the-century American posters, French works from 1896 to 1910, German posters from 1896 to 1936, Art Deco and travel posters, and classic magazine covers
LA

16. Mimi Findlay
10 Father Peter's Lane
New Canaan, CT 06840
203-966-4617
Nineteenth-century interiors and American Victorian furniture

17. Fine Americana
337 East 55 Street
Kansas City, MO 64113
816-523-0330

18. Charles L. Flint Antiques, Inc.
P.O. Box 971
81 Church Street
Lenox, MA 01240
413-637-1634, 413-243-9835
Shaker furniture, oil paintings, folk art, Americana
LA, DLA

19. Patty Gagarin Antiques
    Banks North Road
    Fairfield, CT 06430
    203-259-7332
    Eighteenth- and nineteenth-
    century furniture and folk art
20. Galerie Metropol, Inc.
    927 Madison Avenue
    New York, NY 10021
    212-772-7401
    T
    Twentieth-century furniture and
    crafts by Josef Hoffmann, Kolo
    Moser, Otto Wagner, and
    Adolf Loos
21. Garrison Grey Kingsley
    American Classical Antiques
    P.O. Box 4402
    Greenville, DE 19807
    302-571-8540
    Nineteenth-century Americana
22. Elinor Gordon
    P.O. Box 211
    Villanova, PA 19085
    215-525-0981 (by appointment)
    Chinese Export porcelain
23. Pat Guthman Antiques
    342 Pequot Road
    Southport, CT 06490
    203-259-5743
    Kitchen antiques
24. Kenneth Hammitt Antiques
    Woodbury, CT 06798
    203-263-5676
25. David A. Hanks and Associates
    156 Fifth Avenue
    New York, NY 10010
    212-255-3218
    Late-nineteenth-century furniture
26. Hill Gallery
    163 Townsend
    Birmingham, MI 48011
    313-540-9288
    American folk art, weather vanes,
    whirligigs, and folk sculpture
    TO
27. Industrial Revolution
    P.O. Box 25615
    Chicago, IL 60625
    312-631-0749
    Cy
    Antique advertising art, old
    signs, country-store items, cigar
    labels, fruit-crate art, and old
    metal signs
    MO, LA at $2, DLA

28. Anne Johnson
    American Antiques
    2204 Crestmoor Road
    Nashville, TN 37215
    615-292-6135
29. Margot Johnson, Inc.
    The American-Standard Building
    40 West 40th Street
    New York, NY 10018
    212-840-5472
    V, T
    Late-nineteenth-century American
    antiques
    RO
30. Roland and Marilyn Kemble
    P.O. Box 55
    North Sundale Road
    Norwich, OH 43767
    614-872-3507
    Eighteenth- and nineteenth-
    century American antiques
31. Joseph Kindig
    325 Market Street
    York, PA
    717-848-2760, 717-252-2621
    Eighteenth-century American fur-
    niture and antique European and
    American arms and armor

32. Gerald Kornblau
    790 Madison Avenue
    New York, NY 10021
    212-737-7433
    Folk art
33. Ardis Leigh
    47 State Road
    Princeton, NJ 08540
    609-924-9310
    American eighteenth-century and
    Federal furniture
34. Deanne Levison American
    Antiques and Folk Art
    1933 Peachtree Road, N.E.
    Atlanta, GA 30309
    404-355-0106
    American antiques and folk art
35. Bernard & S. Dean Levy, Inc.
    981 Madison Avenue
    New York, NY 10021
    212-628-7088
    Eighteenth- and early-nineteenth-
    century American furniture,
    paintings, and decorative arts
36. Nathan Liverant & Son
    South Main Street
    Colchester, CT 06415
    203-537-2409
    Eighteenth-century New England
    furniture

37. Made In America
    1234 Madison Avenue
    New York, NY 10028
    212-289-8844
    American quilts (1840–1920),
    formal country furniture,
    nineteenth-century pottery, and
    hooked rugs
    RO
38. Kenneth & Ida Manko Americana
    and Quality Folk Art
    P.O. Box 20
    Moody, ME 04054
    207-646-2595
    Americana and folk art
39. Milly McGehee Americana
    2918 Sale Street
    Dallas, TX 75219
    214-522-8162
    Period antiques and related
    accessories
40. Steve Miller American Folk Art
    17 East 96th Street
    New York, NY 10028
    212-348-5219
    F, AE, V, T
    Antique weather vanes, primitive
    paintings, and American folk
    sculpture
    MO, LA
41. Musgrove Mill Antiques–Prints, Inc.
    509 East St. John Street
    Spartanburg, SC 29302
    803-583-9847
    Prints, paintings, and decorative
    arts of the South
    LA
42. Nimmo & Hart Antiques, Inc.
    Middletown, VT 05757
    802-235-2388
    Eighteenth-century American
    country furniture
43. Ohio Antiques Center, Inc.
    5095 Westerville Road
    Columbus, OH 43229
    614-882-7546
    Eighteenth- and nineteenth-cen-
    tury antiques offered by dealers
    from Ohio, Indiana, Michigan,
    and West Virginia
44. C.L. Prickett
    Stony Hill Road
    Yardley, PA 19067
    215-493-4284
    Eighteenth-century furniture
    from New England, Pennsylva-
    nia, New Jersey, and Maryland

45. Quester Maritime Collection
P.O. Box 446
Stonington, CT 06378
203-535-3860
AE, V, T, Cy
Marine paintings and prints, ship
models, scrimshaw, navigational
instruments, decorative tele-
scopes, etc.
LA at $10

46. Franklin Rappold
18 East Patrick Street
Frederick, MD 21701
301-898-5533, 301-663-6102
Eighteenth-century American
furniture

47. Patricia Anne Reed Fine Antiques
P.O. Box 3704
Tequesta, FL 33458
305-744-0373

48. Ricco-Johnson Gallery
475 Broome Street
New York, NY 10013
212-966-0541
V, T, Cy
American folk art, weather vanes,
sculptures, paintings, and quilts
RO

49. Marguerite Riordan
8 Pearl Street
Stonington, CT 06378
203-535-2511
American primitive painting,
eighteenth-century New England
furniture, and folk art

50. Israel Sack, Inc.
15 East 57th Street
New York, NY 10022
212-753-6562
American furniture from the
seventeenth, eighteenth, and
early-nineteenth centuries

51. Thomas G. Schwenk
956 Madison Avenue
New York, NY 10021
212-772-7222
American antiques

52. Christopher Selser
15 Park Avenue
New York, NY 10016
212-684-5853
Antique American Indian arts

53. Sioux Antiques
8565 Cedar Street
Omaha, NE 68124
402-391-8487

54. David Stockwell, Inc.
P.O. Box 3840
3701 Kennett Pike
Wilmington, DE 19807
302-655-4466
Museum-quality furniture of the
Colonial, Federal, and American
Empire periods

55. Antony Stuempfig
2213 St. James Place
Philadelphia, PA 19103
215-561-7191
American Empire furniture

56. Peter Tillou
Prospect Street
Litchfield, CT 06759
203-567-5706
American nineteenth-century
primitive painting

57. Jonathan Trace
Peekskill Hollow Road
Putnam Valley, NY 10579
914-528-7963
Eighteenth- and nineteenth-cen-
tury American silver and antiques

58. Kenneth and Paulette Tuttle
RFD 4, Box 16
Gardiner, ME 04345
207-582-4496
Country and formal furniture

59. United Art and Antiques
224 Canon Drive
Beverly Hills, CA 90210
213-550-8729
Art Nouveau and Art Deco

60. Robert S. Walin
547 Flanders Road
Woodbury, CT 06798
203-263-4416
C, F, AE
Specializes in "High Country"
Americana

61. John Walton Antiques
P.O. Box 307
Jewett City, CT 06351
203-376-0862
Eighteenth-century New England
country pieces

62. Robert Wieland
33 South St. Andrews Drive
Ormond Beach, FL 32074
904-672-9972
Nineteenth-century and turn-of-
the-century American historical
lithographs
LA

63. I.M. Wiese
Main Street
Southbury, CT 06488
203-354-8911, 203-264-5309
New England furniture and
folk art

64. Jane Wilson
One Hammock Street
Old Saybrook, CT 06475
203-388-9547
Blue and white China Export
(Canton and Nanking) patterns

65. Thomas K. Woodard American
Antiques & Quilts
835 Madison Avenue
New York, NY 10021
212-988-2906
Antique quilts and new textiles

66. Wooton Desk Collection, Inc.
P.O. Box 128
Bayside, NY 11361
212-767-9758
Mid-nineteenth-century furniture
and accessories by American
cabinetmakers, rugs and drapes,
and gas and oil lamps
MO (or contact Richard or
Eileen Dubrow)

Auction Houses

67. E.M. Alexander, Inc.
4410 West 12th
Houston, TX 77055
713-688-5900

68. Antique Resource Center
708 North County Road 18
Minneapolis, MN 55427
612-544-1408

69. Geo. C. Birlant & Co.
191 King Street
Charleston, SC 29401
803-722-3842
F, AE

70. Richard A. Bourne Co., Inc.
P.O. Box 141
Hyannis Port, MA 02647
617-775-0797

71. Bushell's Auction House, Inc.
2006 Second Street
Seattle, WA 98121
206-622-5833

72. Butterfield's
1244 Sutter Street
San Francisco, CA 94109
415-673-1362

73. Chicago Art Galleries, Inc.
1633 Chicago Avenue
Evanston, IL 60201
312-475-6960

74. Christie's
502 Park Avenue
New York, NY 10022
212-546-1000
and
9350 Wilshire Boulevard
Beverly Hills, CA 90024
213-275-5534

75. William Doyle Galleries
175 East 87th Street
New York, NY 10128
212-427-2730

76. Dumouchelle Art Galleries
409 East Jefferson
Detroit, MI 48226
313-936-6255

77. Estate Liquidators Auction
Galleries
4901 East Evans Avenue
Denver, CO 80222
303-753-9111

78. Samuel T. Freeman & Company
1808 Chestnut Street
Philadelphia, PA 19103
215-563-9275

79. Garth's Auctions, Inc.
P.O. Box 369
2690 Stratford Road
Delaware, OH 43015
614-362-4771, 614-369-5085

80. Howard Art Galleries
5100 North Broadway
Chicago, IL 60640
312-271-7100

81. F.B. Hubley & Company, Inc.
364 Broadway
Cambridge, MA 02139
617-876-2030

82. James D. Julia
Skowhegan Road (Route 201)
Fairfield, ME 04937
207-453-9725, 207-453-9493,
207-453-9465

83. Phillips
406 East 79th Street
New York, NY 10021
212-570-4830

84. Selkirk Galleries
4166 Olive Street
St. Louis, MO 63108
314-533-1700

85. Robert W. Skinner, Inc.
Route 117
Bolton, MA 01740
617-779-5528

86. C.G. Sloan & Company, Inc.
919 East Street, N.W.
Washington, D.C. 20004
202-628-1468

87. Sotheby Parke Bernet, Inc.
1334 York Avenue
New York, NY 10021
212-472-3400
and
7660 Beverly Boulevard
Los Angeles, CA 90036
213-937-5130

88. Taylor J. Wayne, Inc.
3848 Bird Road
Miami, FL 33155
305-446-0152

89. Adam A. Weschler & Son, Inc.
905 East Street, N.W.
Washington, D.C. 20004
202-628-1281

90. Helen Winter Associates
P.O. Box 823
21 Cooke Street
Plainville, CT 06062
203-793-0288

Floorcovering

91. The Agèd Ram
P.O. Box 201
Essex, VT 05451
802-878-4530
Cy
Hooked rugs
MO, LA at $2

92. American Olean Tile Company
1000 Cannon Avenue
Lansdale, PA 19446
215-855-1111
Cy
Ceramic tiles

93. Adele Bishop, Inc.
P.O. Drawer 38
Manchester, VT 05254
802-362-3537
C, F, AE, V, Cy
Stencils and related supplies for
floors and walls
MO, RO, LA at $2.50

94. Doris Leslie Blau
15 East 57th Street
New York, NY 10022
212-759-3715
Rugs and carpets

95. Dildarian, Inc.
595 Madison Avenue
New York, NY 10022
212-288-4948
Rugs and carpets

96. Elon, Inc.
P.O. Box 571
642 Sawmill River Road
Ardsley, NY 10502
914-693-8000
Cy
Handmade Mexican, unglazed
terra-cotta tiles

97. Edward Fields, Inc.
232 East 59th Street
New York, NY 10022
212-759-2200
Carpet designs

98. Forms & Surfaces
P.O. Box 5215
Santa Barbara, CA 93108
805-969-4767
Cy
Durable rubber flooring,
including "Bultop"

99. Good Stenciling
P.O. Box 387
Dublin, NH 03444
603-563-8021;
store: 603-880-3480
C, F, AE, V, T, Cy
Handcrafted floorcloths
MO, RO, LA at $2

100. Heritage Rugs
P.O. Box 404
Lahaska, PA 18931
215-794-7229
C
Custom-made, handwoven rugs
MO, RO, LA at 50 cents

101. Jenifer House
New Marlboro Stage
Great Barrington, MA 01230
413-528-1500
Braided, hooked, and rag rugs
MO, RO, LA at 50 cents

102. Jugtown Mountain Rugs
791 Tower Road
Enola, PA 17025
717-323-8703, 717-732-4929
Hand-braided and hand-laced
wool rugs and handloomed wool
rugs
MO, LA at $1

103. Brenda Kellum Stenciling
Commerce, GA 30529
404-335-2087
Stenciling for walls and floors

104. Moravian Pottery and Tile Works
Swamp Road
Doylestown, PA 18901
215-345-6722
Quarry tile, decorative tiles,
and mosaics
LA at $3

105. Mulberry Street Rugs
871 Via de la Paz
Pacific Palisades, CA 90272
213-454-3995; 800-233-0136
Braided and woven rugs
LA at $1 per photo
(refunded with order)

106. Patterson, Flynn & Martin, Inc.
950 Third Avenue
New York, NY 10022
212-751-6414
C, F, AE, V, T, Cy
Custom-woven Savonneries and
hand-tufted rugs, twenty-seven-
inch woven Wiltons and
Axminsters
TO

107. The Rug House
P.O. Box 3042
Cincinnati, OH 45201
513-871-0890
C, F, AE, V, T, Cy
Hand-braided and handwoven
wool rugs
MO, LA at $5

108. Scalamandré Silks, Inc.
950 Third Avenue
New York, NY 10022
212-980-3888
C, F, AE, V, T, Cy
Fabrics, wallpapers, trimmings, and carpets; wallcoverings include reproductions from the Historic Charleston and William Morris collections
TO

109. F. Schumacher & Company, Inc.
939 Third Avenue
New York, NY 10022
212-644-5900
Cy

110. Stark Carpet Corp.
D&D Building
979 Third Avenue
New York, NY 10022
212-752-9000
C, F, AE, V, T, Cy
Rugs and carpets
TO

111. V'Soske Shops, Inc.
155 East 56th Street
New York, NY 10022
212-688-1150
Cy

112. George Wells Rugs, Inc.
565 Cedar Swamp Road
Glen Head, NY 11545
516-676-2056
Custom-made hooked rugs

Furniture

113. Adirondack Store and Gallery
P.O. Drawer 991
Lake Placid, NY 12946
518-523-2646
Specializes in traditional Adirondack lawn chairs

114. Amish Country Collection
RFD 5
Sunset Valley Road
New Castle, PA 16105
412-656-1755
Cy
Amish handcrafted twig furniture, quilts, and rugs
MO, RO, TO, LA at $5

115. Arkitektura
P.O. Box 113
71 East Long Lake Road
Bloomfield Hills, MI 48303
313-646-0097
Cy
Limited edition handcrafted furniture by Eliel Saarinen

116. Artemide, Inc.
150 East 58th Street
New York, NY 10155
212-980-0710
Cy
Features the work of the design group Memphis

117. Atelier International Ltd.
595 Madison Avenue
New York, NY 10022
212-644-0400
Cy
Includes designs by Castiglioni, Le Corbusier, Mackintosh, Rietveld, and Bellini
LA at $2

118. Berea College Student Industries
CPO 2347
Berea, KY 40404
C
Handcrafted reproductions of Early American furniture
LA at $1

119. The Biggs Company
105 East Grace Street
Richmond, VA 23219
F, AE
Reproductions and adaptations of American traditional furniture
LA at $5

120. J&D Brauner
298 Bowery
New York, NY 10012
212-477-2830
Cy
Butcher-block furniture
LA at $1

121. Cabin Creek Furniture
P.O. Box 672
Wake Forest, NC 27587
919-556-1023
C
Handcrafted solid-pine furniture
MO, RO, DLA

122. Castelli Furniture, Inc.
116 Wilbur Place
Bohemia, NY 11716
516-589-0707
Cy
Designs by Pierre Paulin and Charles Pollock

123. City Furniture Company
2200 West 95th Street
Chicago, IL 60643
312-779-6060
Cy
Includes designs by the Memphis group

124. Colonial Clock Company
P.O. Box 813
Kentwood, MI 49508
616-698-8490
C, F, V
Reproduction clocks from Henry Ford Museum, Winterthur Museum, Historic Charleston, and Museum of American Folk Art
MO, RO, DLA, LA at $5 for complete catalog, free brochure

125. Conran's (mail order)
145 Huguenot Street
New Rochelle, NY 10801
914-632-0515
Cy
Contemporary furniture and furnishings
LA at $2.50

126. Cornucopia, Inc.
P.O. Box 44
Westcott Road
Harvard, MA 01451
Handcrafted Windsor chairs, settees, and writing-arm chairs; custom-built cherry and pine dining tables and hutches
LA at $2

127. The Country Loft
South Shore Park
Hingham, MA 02043
617-749-7766; toll-free outside MA: 800-225-5408
C
Furniture and decorative accessories
MO, LA (catalog subscription: $5)

128. Peter Danko Associates, Inc.
917 King Street
Alexandria, VA 22314
703-836-0774
Cy

129. The Davis Round Table
1726 Austell Road
Marietta, GA 30060
404-432-4561
T
Reproduction furniture
RO

130. Deutsch, Inc.
196 Lexington Avenue
New York, NY 10016
Cy
Imported rattan furniture
LA at $2

131. The Dilworthtown Country Store
275 Brintons Bridge Road
West Chester, PA 19380
215-399-0560
C
American country gifts, accessories, and folk art
MO, RO, LA at $2

132. Donghia Associates, Inc.
315 East 62nd Street
New York, NY 10021
212-838-9100
Cy

133. The Door Store
3140 M Street, N.W.
Washington, DC 20007
202-333-7737
Cy
Contemporary furniture and reproductions of classic designs
LA at 50 cents

134. Frederick Duckloe & Bros., Inc.
P.O. Box 427
Portland, PA 18351
717-897-6172
C
Handcrafted Windsor chairs, benches, and rockers
MO, RO, LA at $3

135. The Edison Institute
20900 Oakwood Boulevard
Dearborn, MI 48121
Reproductions from the collections of Greenfield Village and
the Henry Ford Museum
LA at $2.50

136. Emperor Clock Company
Emperor Industrial Park
Fairhope, AL 36532
205-928-2316
C, F
Grandfather-clock kits and fully
assembled and finished clocks;
Queen Anne furniture in kits and
fully assembled
MO, LA at $1

137. Furniture of the
Twentieth Century
154 West 18th Street
New York, NY 10011
212-929-6023
Cy
Designs by Mary Adams, Walter
Chathan, John Danzer, Mariano
Fortuny, Gregory Turpan, and
the Memphis group

138. Guild of Shaker Crafts, Inc.
401 West Savidge Street
Spring Lake, MI 49456
616-846-2870
F, AE
Shaker cherry-wood reproductions
MO, RO, LA at $3.35

139. Guild Woodcrafters of Virginia
P.O. Box 36
Middlebrook, VA 24459
703-885-6575
Reproduction furniture made
to order

140. Historic Charleston Reproductions
P.O. Box 622
105 Broad Street
Charleston, SC 29401
803-723-8292
C, F
Reproductions authorized by the
Historic Charleston Foundation
MO, RO, DLA, LA at $6.50

141. The Hitchcock Chair Company
P.O. Box 507
New Hartford, CT 06057
203-379-8531
C, F
Household Colonial, country,
and traditional furniture

142. Hunt Country Furniture
Webatuck Road
Wingdale, NY 12594
914-832-6522
C, F
Handcrafted interpretations of
American furniture of the
Colonial and Federal periods
MO: P.O. Box 500, Wingdale,
NY 12594; LA at $5 (refunded
with order)

143. Hux-Craft, Inc.
279 East Paces Ferry Road
Atlanta, GA 30305
404-237-1161
Handcrafted white pine reproductions of Early American furniture

144. Vladimir Kagan Designs, Inc.
232 East 59th Street
New York, NY 10022
212-371-1512
Cy

145. Kindel Furniture Company
100 Garden Street, S.E.
Grand Rapids, MI 49507
616-243-3676
Reproductions of furniture from
the Winterthur Museum

146. The Kittinger Company
1893 Elmwood Avenue
Buffalo, NY 14207
716-876-1000
C, F
Reproductions of eighteenth- and
nineteenth-century American furniture from the Williamsburg,
Historic Newport, and Historic
Savannah collections
TO, LA (library catalog $8)

147. Knoll International
The Knoll Building
655 Madison Avenue
New York, NY 10021
212-826-2400
Cy
Designs by Mies van der Rohe,
Marcel Breuer, Richard Meier,
and Robert Venturi

148. The Lane Company
East Franklin Street
Alta Vista, VA 24517
804-369-5641
Traditional reproductions and
contemporary furniture

149. Live Oak Railroad Company
111 East Howard Street
Live Oak, FL 32060
904-362-4419
V
Park benches
MO, LA

150. Magnolia Hall
726 Andover
Atlanta, GA 30327
404-351-1910
V
Victorian and French period
furniture
MO, LA at $1 (80 pages)

151. Herman Miller, Inc.
8500 Bryon Road
Zeeland, MI 49464
616-772-3300
Cy
Designs by Charles Eames and
Eero Saarinen

152. Phyllis Morris Originals
8772 Beverly Boulevard
Los Angeles, CA 90048
213-655-6238
AE, Cy
Design and reproduction furniture, floor lamps, wall sconces,
chandeliers, illuminated cabinets,
and beds
MO, TO, LA at $5

153. The Museum of Modern Art
Store
11 West 53rd Street
New York, NY 10019
212-956-7296
Cy
Reproductions of modern furniture from the museum's design
collection
LA at $1

154. The Pace Collection, Inc.
11–11 34th Avenue
Long Island City, NY 11106
212-721-8201
Cy
Designs by Leon Rosen and
L. Davanzati

155. Palazzetti, Inc.
215 Lexington Avenue
New York, NY 10016
212-684-1199
Cy
Furniture by Mies van der Rohe,
Marcel Breuer, and Le Corbusier
MO, RO, DLA, LA at $1

156. Robinson Iron Corporation
Robinson Road
Alexander City, AL 35010
205-329-8486
V, T
Nineteenth-century cast iron for
the home and garden
RO, TO, DLA, LA at $3

157. The Rocker Shop
P.O. Box 12
Marietta, GA 30061
404-427-2618
V, T, Cy
Rocking chairs and porch swings

158. The Seraph
P.O. Box 500
Route 20
Sturbridge, MA 01566
617-347-2241
C (and country)
Custom-upholstered sofas and
chairs and country accessories
MO, RO, LA at $3

159. Shakertown at Pleasant Hill,
Kentucky
Route 4
Harrodsburg, KY 40330
606-743-5411
V
Shaker furniture, both finished
and kits, baskets, oval boxes,
inspirational drawings, rag rugs,
pegs, and pegrails
MO, RO, LA at 50 cents

160. Shaker Workshops
P.O. Box 1028
Concord, MA 01742
617-646-8985
V
Shaker furniture, both finished
and kits, baskets, oval boxes,
inspirational drawings, rag rugs,
pegs, and pegrails
MO, RO, LA at 50 cents

161. Simms & Thayer, Cabinetmakers
P.O. Box 35
North Marshfield, MA 02059
617-585-8606;
showroom: 617-826-3310
C
Authentic reproductions of
American country furniture
Showroom: 199 Washington St.,
Hanover, MA 02364; MO, RO,
DLA, LA at $3,

162. A. Strader Folk Art Company
100 South Montgomery Street
Union, OH 45322
513-836-6308
F, AE, V
Specializes in folk-art portraits
and children's prints by Arlene
Strader and child-size decorated
and painted furniture
MO, LA at $2, prints available
through some dealers

163. Sunar Ltd.
18 Marshall Street
Norwalk, CT 06854
203-866-3100
Cy

164. Howard Szmolko
P.O. Box 408
Lahaska, PA 18931
215-794-8115
C
Reproductions of eighteenth-
century American furniture
RO

165. Thayer Coggin, Inc.
467 South Road
High Point, NC 27262
919-883-0111

166. Thonet Industries
P.O. Box 1587
491 East Princess Street
York, PA 17405
717-845-6666
Cy

167. Lisa Victoria Brass Beds, Inc.
17106 South Crater Road
Petersburg, VA 23805
804-862-1491
T
Custom-made handcrafted solid-
brass beds
MO

168. Workbench Gallery
470 Park Avenue South
New York, NY 10016
212-532-7900
Cy
The work of furniture makers
from around the country

169. Yesterday's Yankee
Lover's Lane
Lakeville, CT 06039
203-435-9539
C, Cy
Handcrafted furniture reproduc-
tions and accessories and custom-
made contemporary cabinetry
MO, LA

170. Yield House, Inc.
Route 16
North Conway, NH 03860
603-356-3141
Early American and traditional
pine furniture, gifts, and decora-
tive accessories
MO, RO

171. Edward Zucca
P.O. Box 287
R.R. 1 (Park Street)
Putnam, CT 06260
203-928-4380
Cy
Wood furniture

Hardware

172. Baldwin Hardware
Manufacturing Corporation
P.O. Box 82
841 Wyomissing Boulevard
Reading, PA 19603
215-777-7811
C, F, T, Cy
RO, DLA, LA at $2

173. The Country Iron Foundry
P.O. Box 600
Paoli, PA 19301
215-296-7122
C, Cy
Antique, contemporary, and
French firebacks
MO, LA at $1

174. The Essex Forge, Inc.
187 Old Dennison Road
Essex, CT 06426
203-767-1808
C, F
Chandeliers, lanterns, sconces,
firetools, and andirons
RO, LA at $2

175. P.E. Guerin, Inc.
23 Jane Street
New York, NY 10014
212-243-5270
Hardware, bathroom fittings, and
outdoor furniture

176. Heads Up
2980 B Blue Star
Anaheim, CA 92806
714-630-5402
V, T
Oak bathroom furnishings
MO, LA at $1

177. House of Webster
P.O. Box 84
Rogers, AR 72756
501-636-4640
Electric cast-iron ranges, wall
ovens, skillets, and kettles made
from 1875 patterns
MO, LA at 25 cents

178. Lemee's Fireplace Equipment
815 Bedford Street
Bridgewater, MA 02324
617-697-2672
C, V, T, Cy
Fireplace equipment, brass and
copper decorative items, and
wrought-iron and brass hardware
MO, RO, LA at $1

179. Moultrie Manufacturing
Company
P.O. Box 1179
Moultrie, GA 31776
912-985-1312
C, V
Aluminum columns, gates, and
fences and cast-aluminum
furniture
MO, LA at $1

180. Nostalgia
307 Stiles Avenue
Savannah, GA 31401
912-232-2324
Brass and porcelain bathroom
hardware

181. Paxton Hardware Ltd.
7818 Bradshaw Road
Upper Falls, MD 21156
301-592-8505
C, F, AE, V
Fittings, hinges, and banding;
glass shades, bases, candle covers,
Aladdin parts
MO, RO

182. Period Furniture Hardware
Company, Inc.
P.O. Box 314, Charles Street
Station
123 Charles Street
Boston, MA 02114
617-227-0758
Trim, sconces, lanterns, and
trivets

183. The Renovator's Supply
71 Northfield Road
Millers Falls, MA 01349
413-659-2211
C, F, AE, V, T
Decorative hardware, lighting,
plumbing fixtures, textured
wallcoverings, and curtains
MO, RO, LA at $2

184. Ship 'N Out, Inc.
8 Charles Street
Pawling, NY 12564
800-431-8242
T
Brass tubing, fittings, and
fabrications
MO, LA at $1

185. Solebury Forge
205 Airport Road
Doylestown, PA 18901
215-345-7807
Iron light fixtures and accessories,
reproductions from pieces in the
Winterthur Museum

186. South Bound Millworks
P.O. Box 349
Sandwich, MA 02563
617-477-9355
C, V, T, Cy
Wood and wrought-iron curtain
accessories
MO, RO, TO, LA, DLA

187. Strafford Forge
P.O. Box 148
South Strafford, VT 05070
802-765-4455
C, F
Reproductions of architectural
and household hardware of the
Colonial and Federal periods
MO, LA

188. Williamsburg Blacksmiths, Inc.
1 Bultonshop Road
Williamsburg, MA 01096
413-268-7341
C, F, AE
Reproductions of wrought-iron
hardware
MO, RO, LA at $3

Lighting

189. Burdoch Silk Lampshade
Company
11120 Roselle Street, Suite G
San Diego, CA 92121
619-458-1005
V, T
Period reproduction lampshades,
embroidered silk lampshades, and
reproduction bases
MO, RO, LA at $2 (S.A.S.E.)

190. City Lights
2226 Massachusetts Avenue
Cambridge, MA 02140
617-547-1490
V, T
Restored antique lighting,
ca. 1850–1920
RO, LA at $2

191. The Classic Illumination
431 Grove Street
Oakland, CA 94607
415-465-7786
V, T, Cy
Handcrafted lighting fixtures of
solid brass with blown-glass
shades
MO: Ocean View Lighting, 1810
Fourth Street, Berkeley, CA
94710; TO: Classic Illumination,
431 Grove Street, Oakland, CA
94607; LA at $3

192. Hurley Patantee Lighting
RFD 7, Box 98
Kingston, NY 12401

193. Koch & Lowy, Inc.
21–24 39th Avenue
Long Island City, NY 11101
212-786-3520
Cy
Brass fixtures and hand-blown
shades

194. George Kovacs Lighting, Inc.
24 West 40th Street
New York, NY 10018
212-944-9606
Cy
Designs by Robert Sonneman
and others

195. Lightolier, Inc.
346 Claremont Avenue
Jersey City, NJ 07305
201-333-5120
Cy
Contemporary track lighting
and adaptations of oil lamps and
Tiffany shades

196. Luttrells of Lancaster
222 South Broad Street
Lancaster, OH 43130
614-654-9586
Custom-made lampshades
MO, RO, DLA, LA at $2
(refunded with order)

197. Nessen Lamps, Inc.
621 East 216 Street
Bronx, NY 10467
212-231-0221
Cy
Clamp, swing-arm lamps, including designs by Agusti

198. Palmer Hargrave Lamps
P.O. Box 4017
Malibu, CA 90265
213-457-2008
F, Cy
Brass lamps and calfskin shades
TO, LA at $4

199. Paxton Hardware Ltd.
See Hardware

200. Progress Lighting
Erie Avenue and G Street
Philadelphia, PA 19134
215-289-1200
AE, V, T
Reproductions of lighting fix-
tures; chandeliers and matching
brackets
RO, LA at $1

201. Rowe Pottery Works, Inc.
P.O. Box L
217 Main Street
Cambridge, WI 53523
608-423-3935
F
Reproduction nineteenth-century
salt-glaze stoneware and lamp
bases made from jugs, covered
jars, and butter churns
MO, RO, LA at $1.50

202. Roy Electric Company, Inc.
1054 Coney Island Avenue
Brooklyn, NY 11230
212-339-6311
AE, V, T, Cy
MO, RO, DLA, LA at $3

203. Shades of the Past
P.O. Box 502
Corte Madera, CA 94925
V, T
Silk lampshades and antique
brass-base reproductions
MO, LA at $3

204. Stiffel Company
230 Fifth Avenue
New York, NY 10010
212-683-4569
Lighting reproductions from the
Colonial Williamsburg Collection

205. Thunder N Light, Inc.
147 41st Street
Brooklyn, NY 11232
212-499-3777
Cy
Designs by Gae Aulenti and
Centro Stilnovo

206. Victorian Lightcrafters Ltd.
P.O. Box 332
Slate Hill, NY 10973
914-355-1300
V, T
Victorian-style lighting and
wall fixtures
MO, LA at $3

Miscellaneous Accessories

207. Art Poster Company
22255 Greenfield Road, Suite 142
Southfield, MI 48075
313-559-1230; order department:
800-521-8634
C, AE, Cy
Art posters and prints
MO, RO, LA at $2

208. Phyllis Aycock
2 Adrian Avenue, Apt. 37A
Bronx, New York 10463
212-562-5380
Original folk art: Early American
primitive-style portraits, landscapes, and still lifes
LA at $1.50, commission: photos
of paintings mailed to interested
clients; arrangements made by
mail, phone, or in person

209. John Morgan Baker—Framer
P.O. Box 149
210 Hardy Way
Worthington, OH 43085
614-885-7040
C, F, AE, V
Custom-made frames of solid
curly or bird's-eye maple
MO, LA (S.A.S.E.); 40 cents in
stamps for color photos, if desired

210. The Boston Museum of Fine
Arts Shop
P.O. Box 1044
Boston, MA 02120
617-427-1111; toll-free outside
Massachusetts: 800-225-5592

211. Canvasback Art Company, Inc.
Jones River Park
Kingston, MA 02364
617-585-4550
C
Reproductions of oil paintings
from the Museum of American
Folk Art and the Winterthur
Museum
MO, LA at $1

212. Coker Creek Crafts &
Handweavers
P.O. Box 95
Coker Creek, TN 37314
615-261-2157
V, Cy
Handmade split white-oak bas-
kets and handwoven place mats,
rugs, and table-runners

213. Colonial Williamsburg
P.O. Box CH
Williamsburg, VA 23187
800-446-9240

214. Don Darragh Country & Shaker
Collectables
P.O. Box 81
Springfield, TN 37172
615-384-4392
C, AE
Country and Shaker decorative
pieces in wood
MO, LA at $2 (refunded with
order)

215. The Decoy Works
2601 S.W. 122nd Avenue
Davie, FL 33330
305-472-7910
V, T, Cy
Reproductions of antique shorebird and duck decoys and wooden
signs with bird and duck motifs
MO, RO, DLA, LA

216. Good Directions Company
24 Ardmore Road
Stamford, CT 06902
203-348-1836
Reproductions of copper and
brass weather vanes
MO

217. Heritage Hall Prints
P.O. Box 241
Old Agency Road
Ridgeland, MS 39157
601-856-4082
C, F, AE, V, T, Cy
Open and limited edition prints
from original paintings of
primitive-style portraits, genre,
and still lifes
MO, RO, LA at $2

218. Kennedy Galleries, Inc.
40 West 57th Street
New York, NY 10019
212-541-9600
American prints and paintings of
all periods

219. Will Kirkpatrick Shorebird
Decoys, Inc.
124 Forest Avenue
Hudson, MA 01749
617-562-7841
Hand-carved, painted reproductions of early shorebird and duck
decoys and songbirds
MO, RO, LA at $1

220. Metropolitan Museum of Art
Fifth Avenue and 82nd Street
New York, NY 10028
212-535-7710

221. Mottahedeh and Company, Inc.
225 Fifth Avenue
New York, NY 10010
212-685-3050
C, F, AE
Reproduction Chinese Export
and European porcelain dinnerware and accessories; reproduction accessories in brass; represents the Winterthur Museum,
the Historic Charleston Foundation, and the Metropolitan
Museum of Art
RO, LA
The Museum of Modern Art
Store
See Furniture

222. New Geneva Stoneware
P.O. Box 649
Liberty Street
Masontown, PA 15461
412-583-2170
V, T
Traditionally crafted stoneware
pottery
MO, LA at $1 (refunded
with order)

223. The Old Print Shop
150 Lexington Avenue
New York, NY 10016
212-683-3950
American prints and paintings

224. Old Sturbridge Village
Museum Gift Shop
Sturbridge, MA 01566
617-347-3362
A range of gift merchandise
MO, LA

225. Max Protetch Gallery
37 West 57th Street
New York, NY 10019
212-838-2340
Michael Graves silver designs
manufactured by Alessi of Milan

226. Sarsaparilla Deco Designs Limited
5711 Washington Street
West New York, NJ 07093
201-863-8002
Art Deco lamps and glassware

227. Stencil School
P.O. Box 94
Shrewsbury, MA 01545
617-845-9440, 617-845-2440
C, Cy
Original design country stencils,
handmade accessories, wooden-
ware, and fabricware
MO, RO, LA at $1

228. Tin Wishes
P.O. Box 181
Youngsville, PA 16371
814-563-4919
Hand-cut antiqued tin silhouettes
of "country" shapes
MO

229. Williamsburg Reproductions
Colonial Williamsburg
Williamsburg, VA 23185
804-229-1000

230. Winterthur Reproductions
Winterthur Museum and
Gardens
Winterthur, DE 19735
800-441-8229

Paints and Wallpapers

231. Benchmark Wallcoverings
Decorative Projects Division
National Gypsum Company
10 New England Executive Park
Burlington, MA 01803
617-273-4900

232. Bradbury & Bradbury Wallpapers
P.O. Box 155
Benicia, CA 94510
707-746-1900
V
Hand-printed Victorian borders
and wallpapers; Victorian friezes,
borders, rosettes, dadoes, and
corner fans
MO, LA at $1

233. Brunschwig & Fils
D&D Building
979 Third Avenue
New York, NY 10022
212-838-7878
C, F, AE, V, T, Cy
Fabrics and wallpapers, including
reproductions of objects in the
Cooper-Hewitt Collection and
the Winterthur Museum
RO

234. Clarence House
40 East 57th Street
New York, NY 10022
212-752-2890
C, F, AE, V, T, C
Seventeenth-, eighteenth-, and
nineteenth-century fabric designs;
eighteenth- and nineteenth-
century wallpapers
TO

235. Collins & Aikman Corp.
23645 Mercantile Road
Cleveland, OH 44122
216-464-3700
Cy
Contract wallcoverings

236. Columbus Coated Fabrics
Division of Borden Chemical
1280 North Grant Avenue
Columbus, OH 43126
614-225-6167
Includes Wall-Tex and Imperial
Wallcovering lines

237. Devoe Paint Division
4000 Du Pont Circle
Louisville, KY 40207
502-589-9340

238. Fuller-O'Brien Paints
P.O. Box 864
2700 Glynn Avenue
Brunswick, GA 31521
912-265-7650
C, F, AE, V
Heritage color collection (Colonial colors); Cape May Victorian
color palette
RO, LA: Heritage collection card
available at no charge; Victorian
color palette available at $1.50

239. Greef Fabrics, Inc.
155 East 56th Street
New York, NY 10022
212-751-0200
Includes the Shelburne Museum
Collection

240. GTR Wallcovering Company
Division of General Tire &
Rubber Company
401 Hackensack Avenue
Hackensack, NJ 07601
201-489-0100
Includes Fashon Wallcovering line

241. The Hinson Collections
251 Park Avenue South
New York, NY 10010
212-475-4100
Features patterns from the American Wing of the Metropolitan Museum of Art

242. Katzenbach & Warren
950 Third Avenue
New York, NY 10022
Colonial Williamsburg wallpapers

243. Milbrook, Inc.
Division of Imperial Wallcoverings
23645 Mercantile Road
Cleveland, OH 44122
216-464-3700
Features wallpaper designs from the Museum of American Folk Art

244. The Old-Fashioned Milk Paint Company
P.O. Box 222
Groton, MA 01450
617-448-6336

245. Pittsburgh Paints
1 Gateway Center
Pittsburgh, PA 15222
412-434-3131
Scalamandré Silks, Inc.
See Floorcovering
F. Schumacher & Company, Inc.
See Floorcovering

246. Martin Senour Company
1370 Ontario Avenue
Cleveland, OH 44113
Includes the Williamsburg paint collection

247. Stencil House
RFD 9, Box 287
Concord, NH 03301
603-225-9121
C, F, AE, V
Stencils on Mylar, cut and uncut
MO, LA at $2, wholesale inquiries considered

248. Richard E. Thibaut, Inc.
706 South 21st Street
Irvington, NJ 07111
201-399-7888
Includes Historic House Association of America Collection

249. Albert Van Luit, Inc.
4000 Chevy Chase Drive
Los Angeles, CA 90039
213-247-8840
Textile reproductions from the Winterthur Collection
Waverly Fabrics
See Floorcovering

Textiles

250. Laura Ashley
714 Madison Avenue
New York, NY 10021
212-371-0099
Cy
Floral and geometric prints
Brunschwig & Fils
See Paints and Wallpapers

251. Constance Carol, Inc.
P.O. Box 899
Cordage Park
Plymouth, MA 02360
617-746-6116
C, F, V, T, Cy
Tab curtains, other traditional curtains, and related products
MO, LA: catalog, $1; catalog and swatches, $5
Clarence House
See Paints and Wallpapers

252. Country Curtains
Stockbridge, MA 01262
413-243-1805
C, F, V, T, Cy
Curtains in cotton, muslin, and permanent press. Ruffles, tab styles, lined and unlined Waverly and Schumacher curtains, bed ensembles, tablecloths, pillows, and dolls
MO, RO, LA

253. Dorothy's Ruffled Originals, Inc.
6721 Market Street
Wilmington, NC 28405
919-791-1296; toll free: 800-334-2593; toll free in North Carolina: 800-672-2947
V, T
Custom-made ruffled curtains and accessories
MO, RO, LA at $4

254. Fieldcrest Mills Inc.
60 West 40th Street
New York, NY 10018
212-536-1200

255. Homespun Crafts
P.O. Box 1776
Blacksburg, SC 29702
704-937-7611
C, V, T
MO, RO, LA at $1

256. Homespun Weavers
530 State Avenue
Emmaus, PA 18049
215-967-4550
C
Cotton fabrics for tablecloths, bedspreads, and drapes; custom-made tablecloths and cotton kitchen towels
MO, RO (factory store at 530 State Avenue), LA (S.A.S.E.), DLA

257. Mrs. Sheldon Howe
4 Lorita Lane
Northfield, MA 01360
413-498-2007
V
Custom-made fishnet canopies for highpost beds

258. Lee Joffa, Inc.
800 Central Boulevard
Carlstadt, NJ 07072
201-438-8444
C, F, V, T, Cy
Textiles, wallcoverings, traditional and contemporary upholstery

259. Jack Lenor Larsen
41 East 11th Street
New York, NY 10003
212-674-3993
Cy

260. Ralph Lauren Home Collection
1185 Avenue of the Americas
New York, NY 10036
212-930-2380

261. Marimekko
7 West 56th Street
New York, NY 10019
212-581-9616
Cy

262. Patchcraft
P.O. Box 657
Dorset, VT 05251
802-867-5307
Scalamandré Silks, Inc.
See Floorcovering
F. Schumacher & Company, Inc.
See Floorcovering

263. Springs Industries, Inc.
Consumer Fashion Division
104 West 40th Street
New York, NY 10018
212-556-6000

264. Standard Trimming Company
1114 First Avenue
New York, NY 10022
212-755-3034
C, F, AE, V, T, Cy
Tiebacks, trimming, cords, and tassels

265. J.P. Stevens & Company, Inc.
Stevens Tower
1185 Avenue of the Americas
New York, NY 10036
212-930-2000

266. Stroheim and Roman
10 West 20th Street
New York, NY 10011
212-691-0700
Reproductions of upholstery and drapery fabrics based on those in the Winterthur Collection
Sunar Ltd.
See Furniture
Albert Van Luit, Inc.
See Paints and Wallpapers
Waverly Fabrics
See Floorcovering

267. West Point Pepperell/Martex
1221 Avenue of the Americas
New York, NY 10018
212-382-5000

268. Wilson's, Inc.
258 Main Street
Greenfield, MA 01301
413-774-4326
C
Tobacco cloth
MO

Selected Bibliography

Decorative Arts by Style Periods

Anscombe, Isabelle, and Gere, Charlotte. *Arts and Crafts in Britain and America.* New York: Rizzoli International Publications, 1978.

Bacot, H. Parrot. *Southern Furniture and Silver: The Federal Period, 1788–1830.* Baton Rouge, La.: Anglo-American Art Museum, 1968.

The Baltimore Museum of Art. *Maryland Queen Anne and Chippendale Furniture of the Eighteenth Century.* Baltimore, Md.: Baltimore Museum of Art, 1968.

Battersby, Martin. *The World of Art Nouveau.* New York: Funk & Wagnalls, 1968.

Battersby, Martin. *The Decorative Twenties.* New York: Walker, 1969.

Battersby, Martin. *The Decorative Thirties.* New York: Walker, 1971.

Bishop, Robert, and Coblentz, Patricia. *The World of Antiques, Art, and Architecture in Victorian America.* New York: E.P. Dutton, 1979.

Bridenbaugh, Carl. *The Colonial Craftsman.* Chicago and London: University of Chicago Press, 1974.

The Brooklyn Museum. *The American Renaissance: 1876–1917.* New York: Brooklyn Museum, 1979.

Butler, Joseph T. *American Antiques 1800–1900: A Collector's History and Guide.* New York: Odyssey Press, 1965.

Cathers, David M. *Furniture of the American Arts and Crafts Movement: Stickley and Roycroft Mission Oak.* New York: New American Library, 1981.

Chippendale, Thomas. *The Gentleman and Cabinet-Maker's Director.* New York: Dover Publications, reprint 1966.

Clark, Robert Judson, ed. *The Arts and Crafts Movement in America, 1876–1916.* Princeton, N.J.: Princeton University Press, 1972.

Colonial Williamsburg Foundation. *The Williamsburg Collection of Antique Furnishings.* Williamsburg, Va.: Colonial Williamsburg Foundation, 1973.

Downs, Joseph. *American Furniture—Queen Anne and Chippendale Periods.* New York: Macmillan, 1962.

Duncan, Alastair. *Art Nouveau and Art Deco Lighting.* New York: Simon and Schuster, 1978.

Elder, William Voss, III. *Baltimore Painted Furniture 1800–1840.* Baltimore, Md.: Baltimore Museum of Art, 1972.

Garner, Philippe. *Contemporary Decorative Arts from 1940 to the Present.* New York: Facts on File, 1980.

Garner, Philippe, ed. *The Encyclopedia of Decorative Arts: 1890–1940.* New York: Van Nostrand Reinhold, 1979.

Garrett, Elisabeth Donaghy. *American Interiors: Colonial and Federal Periods.* New York: Crown Publishers, 1980.

Garrett, Elisabeth Donaghy, comp. *The Antiques Book of Victorian Interiors.* New York: Crown Publishers, 1981.

Garrett, Wendell D. *The Arts in America: The Nineteenth Century.* New York: Charles Scribner's Sons, 1969.

Grand Rapids Museum. *Renaissance Revival Furniture.* Grand Rapids, Mich.: Grand Rapids Museum, 1976.

Greif, Martin. *Depression Modern: The Thirties Style in America.* New York: Universe Books, 1975.

Grow, Lawrence. *The Catalogue of Contemporary Design.* New York: Collier Books, 1983.

Howe, Katherine S., and Warren, David B. *The Gothic Revival Style in America, 1830–1870.* Houston: Museum of Fine Arts, 1976.

Kenney, John Tarrant. *The Hitchcock Chair: The Story of a Connecticut Yankee— L. Hitchcock of Hitchcocks-ville—and an Account of the Restoration of This 19th Century Manufactory.* New York: Clarkson N. Potter, 1971.

Kirk, John T. *American Chairs: Queen Anne and Chippendale.* New York: Alfred A. Knopf, 1972.

Kirk, John T. *Early American Furniture.* New York: Alfred A. Knopf, 1974.

Madigan, Mary Jean, ed. *Nineteenth Century Furniture: Innovation, Revival and Reform.* New York: Billboard Publications, 1982.

Meadmore, Clement. *The Modern Chair: Classics in Production.* New York: Van Nostrand Reinhold, 1979.

The Metropolitan Museum of Art. *Nineteenth Century America: Furniture and Other Decorative Arts.* New York: Metropolitan Museum of Art, 1970.

Montgomery, Charles F. *American Furniture: The Federal Period, 1788–1825.* New York: Viking Press, 1966.

The Newark Museum. *Classical America 1815–1845.* Newark, N.J.: The Newark Museum, 1963.

Otto, Celia Jackson. *American Furniture of the Nineteenth Century.* New York: Viking Press, 1965.

Pool, Mary Jane. *20th-Century Decorating, Architecture and Gardens.* New York: Holt, Rinehart, and Winston, 1980.

Schwartz, Marvin D., Stanek, Edward J., and True, Douglas K. *The Furniture of John-Henry Belter and the Rococo Revival: An Inquiry into Nineteenth-Century Furniture Design Through a Study of the Gloria and Richard Manney Collection.* New York: E.P. Dutton, 1981.

Sheraton, Thomas. *Cabinet-Maker's and Upholsterer's Drawing Book.* New York: Dover Publications, 1972.

Sprigg, June. *By Shaker Hands.* New York: Alfred A. Knopf, 1975.

Steinfeldt, Cecilia, and Stover, Donald Lewis. *Early Texas Furniture and Decorative Arts.* San Antonio, Tex.: Trinity University Press, 1973.

Tracy, Berry B., Shwartz, Marvin D., and Boorsch, Suzanne. *19th-Century America: Furniture and Other Decorative Arts, An Exhibition in Celebration of the Hundredth Anniversary of The Metropolitan Museum of Art.* New York: Metropolitan Museum of Art, 1970.

Architecture

Andrews, Wayne. *Pride of the South: A Social History of Southern Architecture.* New York: Atheneum, 1979.

Blumenson, John J. *Identifying American Architecture: A Pictorial Guide to Styles and Terms, 1600–1945.* Nashville, Tenn.: American Association for State and Local History, 1977.

Johnson, Philip C. *Mies van der Rohe.* Boston: Museum of Modern Art/New York Graphic Society, 1978.

Millar, John Fitzhugh. *The Architects of the American Colonies.* Barre, Mass.: Barre Publishers, 1968.

Nichols, F.D. *The Architecture of Georgia,* rev. ed. Savannah, Ga.: Beehive Press, 1976.

Poppeliers, John, Chambers, S. Allen, and Schwartz, Nancy B. *What Style Is It?* Washington, D.C.: Preservation Press, 1984.

Rifkind, Carole. *A Field Guide to American Architecture.* New York: New American Library, 1980.

Walker, Lester. *American Shelter: An Illustrated Encyclopedia of the American Home.* Woodstock, N.Y.: Overlook Press, 1981.

Weslager, C.A. *The Log Cabin in America.* New Brunswick, N.J.: Rutger's University Press, 1969.

Decorating

Conran, Terence. *The House Book.* New York: Crown Publishers, 1976.

Conran, Terence. *The Bed and Bath Book.* New York: Crown Publishers, 1978.

Emmerling, Mary Ellisor. *American Country: A Style and Source Book.* New York: Clarkson N. Potter, 1980.

Grow, Lawrence, comp. *The Third Old House Catalogue.* New York: Collier Books, 1982.

Kron, Joan, and Slesin, Suzanne. *High-Tech: The Industrial Style and Source Book for the Home.* New York: Clarkson N. Potter, 1978.

Labine, Clem, and Flaherty, Carolyn, eds. *The Old-House Journal Compendium.* Woodstock, N.Y.: Overlook Press, 1980.

Lynn, Catherine. *Wallpaper in America: From the Seventeenth Century to World War I.* New York: W. W. Norton, 1980.

Mayhew, Edgar de N., and Myers, Minor, Jr. *A Documentary History of American Interiors: From the Colonial Era to 1915.* New York: Charles Scribner's Sons, 1980.

Nylander, Jane C. *Fabrics for Historic Buildings.* Washington, D.C.: Preservation Press, 1984.

Nylander, Richard C. *Wall Papers for Historic Buildings.* Washington, D.C.: Preservation Press, 1984.

Seale, William. *Recreating the Historic House Interior.* Nashville, Tenn.: American Association for State and Local History, 1979.

Seale, William. *The Tasteful Interlude: American Interiors Through the Camera's Eye, 1860–1917.* New York: E.P. Dutton, 1981.

Stoddard, Alexandra. *Style for Living: How to Make Where You Live You.* Garden City, N.Y.: Doubleday, 1974.

Waites, Raymond, Martin, Bettye, and Skurka, Norma. *American View: Color Your Home Beautiful with Country Colors, Patterns and Forms.* New York: Harper & Row, 1984.

Wellikoff, Alan. *The American Historical Supply Catalogue: A Nineteenth Century Sourcebook.* New York: Schocken Books, 1984.

Wilson, José, and Leaman, Arthur. *The Second Complete Home Decorating Catalogue.* New York: Holt, Rinehart and Winston, 1981.

General Antiques

Comstock, Helen. *American Furniture: Seventeenth, Eighteenth, and Nineteenth Century Styles.* New York: Viking Press, 1962.

Comstock, Helen. *The Concise Encyclopedia of American Antiques.* New York: Hawthorn Books, 1965.

Davidson, Marshall B. *Three Centuries of Amerian Antiques.* New York: Bonanza Books, 1979.

Fairbanks, Jonathan L., and Bates, Elizabeth Bidwell. *American Furniture 1620 to the Present.* New York: Richard Marek Publishers, 1981.

Fales, Dean A., Jr., and Bishop, Robert. *American Painted Furniture 1660–1880.* New York: E.P. Dutton, 1972.

Kirk, John T. *The Impecunious Guide to American Antiques.* New York: Alfred A. Knopf, 1975.

Kopp, Joel, and Kopp, Kate. *American Hooked and Sewn Rugs: Folk Art Underfoot.* New York: E.P. Dutton, 1975.

Little, Nina Fletcher. *Floor Coverings in New England Before 1850.* Sturbridge, Mass.: Old Sturbridge Village, 1972.

Morton, Robert. *Southern Antiques and Folk Art.* Birmingham, Ala.: Oxmoor House, 1976.

Naeve, Milo M. *Identifying American Furniture.* Nashville, Tenn.: American Association for State and Local History, 1981.

Nutting, Wallace. *Furniture Treasury.* New York: Macmillan, 1954.

Peirce, Donald, and Alswang, Hope. *American Interiors: New England and the South.* New York: Brooklyn Museum, 1983.

Poesch, Jessie. *The Art of the Old South: Painting, Sculpture, Architecture & the Products of Craftsmen, 1560–1860.* New York: Alfred A. Knopf, 1983.

Schwartz, Marvin D. *American Interiors, 1675–1885: A Guide to the American Period Rooms in the Brooklyn Museum.* New York: Brooklyn Museum, 1968.

Smith, Carter. *Country Antiques and Collectibles: How to Find Them, Where to Buy Them, How to Decorate with Them.* Birmingham, Ala.: Oxmoor House, 1981.

Acknowledgements

Books are, by their nature, communal undertakings; for the author of a heavily pictorial book such as *Decorating with Americana*, this is, perhaps, the most rewarding aspect of the work. It's not just the fun of collaborating with creative people, but also in how much one learns from each of the skilled professionals involved in a complicated book: architects, designers, consultants, photographers, editors, book designers, compositors, marketing people, and on and on.

Closest to home, at Media Projects, I want particularly to thank Bruce Glassman, Assistant Editor, who filled several roles with skill and dedication. Ellen Coffey, Frank Kurtz, Jeffrey Woldt, Julie Colmore, Nancy Lorenz, Maureen Crowley, and Ann Ivins also contributed importantly at MPI.

Alexandra Stoddard, interior designer and writer, has shown great flair and down-to-earth practicality in her essay, and she has been a joy to work with once again.

The design of the book is the work of Michael Shroyer, both a gifted designer and an amiable problem solver.

Allison Eckardt of *The Magazine Antiques,* has my deepest gratitude for her instructive review of the text and her many creative suggestions.

Our colleagues at Oxmoor House have, as in the past, been highly supportive and professionally deft. Our thanks go to our editors, Karen Irons and John Logue; in production to Jerry Higdon, Jane Bonds, and Jim Thomas; in marketing to Don Logan, Tom Angelillo, Diane Mooney, Steve Logan, and Fred Burk. (We also acknowledge with thanks the contributions of Oxmoor House's marketing suppliers Dick Long, Linda Wells, and Jack Walsh.)

We are greatly in debt to many generously cooperative homeowners for their gracious assistance. These are: Mr. and Mrs. John Newton Wall; Robert Fowler; Mr. and Mrs. George Considine; William Adams Jr., Alan Minge, David Stockwell, Mr. and Mrs. Lawrence Conklin; Alexandra Stoddard; Reverend and Mrs. Alanson Houghton; Mr. and Mrs. Theodore Lamont Cross (interior designer Mary Cross); Mr. and Mrs. David Stockwell; Mr. Daniel Huger; Erica Wilson and Vladimir Kagen; Mrs. Carter Smith; Mr. and Mrs. Sligh Rutherford; Mr. and Mrs. Richard Jennerette; Mrs. Shirley Reed Self; Mr. and Mrs. David Andrews; Mr. Christopher Forbes; Phillip Johnson; Mr. and Mrs. Richard Maltby; Mrs. Duncan Ellsworth; Dee Dee and Jim Lee; Carolyn Tynes; Leon and Sue Potts.

It is a pleasure to gratefully acknowledge the contributions of the following photographers; Herbert K. Barnett, p. 147; Paul Beswick, cover, pp. 2–3, 8, 25, 178, 180, 181, 182, 183; Lee Boltin, pp. 62, 65, 98; George W. Gardner, pp. 172, 173; Bruce Glassman, pp. 174, 192, 193; David Goldberg, pp. 24, 66, 67, 68, 69, 70, 71, 72, 73, 139; Helga Studio (Arthur Vitols) pp. 32–43, 48–54, 84–86, 90–96, 102, 103, 140, 141, 152, 154, 155, 157; Mac Jamieson, pp. 130, 131, 135; June Kuefler, p. 146; Bob Lancaster, pp. 64, 78, 114, 120, 165, 169; Martha Porter, pp. 105, 106, 202, 203; Brad Rauschenberg; Carter Smith, pp. 6, 7, 44, 66, 81, 96, 97, 100, 104, 115, 116, 125, 132, 138, 139, 159, 160, 163; Alexandra Stoddard; Roy Thigpen, pp. 82, 83; Samuel White, p. 164; Herbert Wise, pp. 9, 17, 19, 148, 150, 179, 184; Jimmy Jack Wall p. 182; Betsy Swanson, pp. 78, 100; Gary Parker, p. 135, 165, 169; John O'Hagan, pp. 27, 171, back-jacket (couch); Peter Sanders, p. 26; Brad Oldenberg, pp. 31, 32; Otto Nelson, pp. 155–157.

Finally, the author is also very grateful to a number of individuals, institutions, staffs of historic houses, and corporations who were particularly helpful to us: Charles K. Driscoll, Susan Bruno—*Colonial Williamsburg Foundation*; Catherine H. Maxwell, Alberta M. Brandt, Karol A. Schmiegal—*Winterthur Museum*; Allison Harwood—*Historic Charleston Foundation*; François Poulet, Laurie Lebo—*Museum of Fine Arts Boston*; Kevin Staton, Glenda Galt—*The Brooklyn Museum*; Lois Emma—*The Metropolitan Museum of Art*; *The Historic Savannah Foundation*; Jane Brown—*Shakertown, Pleasant Hill, Kentucky*; *Museum of Early Southern Decorative Arts*; John Gerard—*The Cranbrook Academy of Art*; *The Conde-Charlotte House*; Sarah Callander—*Laura Ashley, Inc.*; Adriana Bitter—*Scalamandré; Imperial Wallcoverings*; Frances Wise—*Ruder, Finn & Rotman*; Carl Ruff, Linda Folland—*Herman Miller*; Don Rorke, Amelia Peck—*Knoll International*; Christine Rae—*Sunar*; Bevin Sloan—*Rockefeller Center, Inc.*; *Radio City Music Hall*; Al Vittum, Susan M. Valenti—*Monroe Federal Savings Bank*; David B. Martin—*Patterson, Flynn & Martin*; Margot Dockrell—*Brunschwig & Fils*; Robert Herring—*Schumacher*; Nancy Cote—*Johnson and Burgee*; Michael Graves; Letitia Baldrige, Page Kjellstrom—*Letitia Baldrige Enterprises, Inc.*; Cornelia Pelzer, Lorraine C. Van Inwegan—*Sign of the Phoenix*; Ginger Sawyer—*Robert W. Skinner, Inc.*; Cintra H. Huber—*Phillips*; Lisa Newsom—*Southern Accents*; Dianne Goodner, Roy Overcast—*Decorating and Craft Ideas*; William Doyle, Neysa Furey—*William Doyle Galleries*; Nina Klippel—*Creamer, Dickson, and Basford, Inc.*; Marilyn Lehman—*Frank Lloyd Wright Home and Studio Foundation*; Barbara Morgan—*Springs, Inc.*; Rose Gerace—*J.P. Stevens, Inc.*; Phillip Leif—*Phillip Leif Associates*; Marcia Hamburger—*Echo Antiques*; Ed Haleman—*Stark Carpet Corp.*; *Museum of American Folk Art*; *Richard and Eileen Dubrow Antiques*; Brenda McCauley—*Stiffel Co.*; *Fieldcrest*; Nancy B. Emerson—*Virginia Division of Tourism*; Mary Lee Allen, Ben Brown—*The Friends of Gunston Hall*; *George Wells Rugs*; Martha Mackie—*Cabin Creek Furniture*; Cindy Martin, Vikki Fulop—*Ralph Lauren Home Collection*; *West Point Pepperell/Martex*; Dale A. Neseman—*Kittinger Corp.*; Lilitia Bergs—*Old Sturbridge Village*; *Simms & Thayer*; Beth DeWall—*Cincinnati Art Museum*; Ellen Kelly Ritchie, Mark Gompertz—*Overlook Press*; *Christie's*; John Pugmire; Melissa McGinnis, Lynne Arden—*Arlington Antebellum Home*; Joan Stuart Neave—*Patchcraft*; Joanne Cheek—*American Antiques*; Cecile Carr—*Hitchcock Chair Co.*; *The John T. Kenny Hitchcock Museum*; Robert Bishop—*Museum of American Folk Art*; *Taliesen*; *The Nathaniel Russell House, The Stanley-Whitman House*; *Houston Antique Museum*; *Madame John's Legacy*; *Old Merchant's House*; *The Bartow-Pell Mansion*; *Oakleigh*, Mr. and Mrs. John Callon—*Melrose* (Linda Reed, interior designer); *Center for Music, Drama, and Art, Lake Placid, New York*; *Constance Carol, Inc.*; *Hurley Patentee Manor*; *A. Strader Folk Art Co.*; *Yesterday's Yankee*; *Lemee's Fireplace Equipment*; *Rug House*; *Good Directions*; Don Darragh; *Classic Illumination*; *Shades of the Past*; *The Agèd Ram*; *Amish Country Store*; *The Rocker Shop*; Will Kirkpatrick, founder of *Shorebird Decoys, Inc.*; *Heads Up*; *Art Poster Company*; *Sarsaparilla Deco Designs Ltd.*; *George Kovacs Lighting*; *Castelli Furniture*; *Forms and Surfaces*; and Ann Nathews of *Oxmoor House.*

Resource Guide photo credits: Wooton desk, p. 208: Richard and Eileen Dubrow—Wooton Desk Collection [R.G. #66]. Horse weather vane, p. 209: Steve Miller—American Folk Art [R.G. #40]. Victorian "Topiary Stripe" wallpaper, p. 210: Wall-Tex Matchmaker's Collection [R.G. #236]. Horse and jockey, p. 211: Ellen Page Wilson—Ricco-Johnson Gallery [R.G. #48]. Chair, p. 212: Arkitektura [R.G. #115]. Windsor chair, p. 213: Howard Szmolko [R.G. #164]. Gargoyle, p. 214: Robinson Iron [R.G. #156]. Cow clock, p. 214: Colonial Clock Company [R.G. #124]. Eagle weather vane, p. 215: Ricco-Johnson Gallery [R.G. #48]. Lounge chair, p. 217: Arkitektura [R.G. #115].

Index

Accessories
  bathroom furnishings, 176; box
  lock, 26; candle extinguisher, 140;
  chair rail, 142; coat and hat rack,
  157; door knocker, 160; doorstops,
  138, 160; deed box, 87; gameboards,
  country, 176; gun case, 153; hall
  tree, 124; hat hanger, 137; inkstand,
  158; pole screen, 53; planter boxes,
  56; punkah fan, 118; umbrella stand,
  124; wastebasket, 157; wicker
  planter, 128; wooden bowl, 135;
  yarn swift, 142
Adam, Robert, 59, 61, 88
Advertising, twentieth-century, 18
African influence, 182
American classic style, 182
Amish furnishings, 26, 72, 176
Andirons, metal, 68
Art—see also paintings and portraits,
  posters and prints
  bust, 92; crab, 158; crucifix, 17, 86;
  eagle, 51; engravings, 42; folk
  carvings, 18, 51, 133, 158; hunting
  dogs, 161; mural, 190; photographs,
  137; plaster sculpture, 172; Spanish
  Colonial religious, 84
Art Deco style, 182, 188, 191, 192,
  193, 195, 206
Art Moderne style, 182

Art Nouveau style, 156, 159, 172, 173,
  175, 176
Arts and Crafts movement, 156
Askins, Norman D., 179
Aztec Indians, 182

Baskets, 68, 74, 134, 168
Bauhaus design school, 182
Bed, 127, 176
  bedstead, 74; brass, 127; cupboard, 74;
  daybed, 32, 48; Deco style, 206;
  four-poster, 72; metal, 127, 158;
  oak, 158; painted, 42, 170;
  pencil-post, 183; pine, 106, 183;
  "rice," 62, 63; sleigh, 88, 97;
  tall-post, 42, 51, 74; tester, 47, 119
Bed furnishings, 42, 51, 53, 97, 139,
  206
Belter, John Henry, 116, 119, 120
Bench, garden, 56, 140 (red painted)
Bertoia, Harry, 199
Blankets, 13, 86, 133, 165—see also
  quilts and coverlets
Bookcases, 75, 86, 92, 99, 111, 124,
  151, 181, 193, 203
Boxes, 16, 42, 51, 75, 82, 87, 126,
  140, 141, 142, 181
Braque, Georges, 182
Breuer, Marcel, 179, 185, 203, 206,
  207
Buckland, William, 31

Cabinetmakers, 12, 56, 191
Cabinets, 77, 112 (pie safe), 114, 150,
  158, 168, 191
Candlestands, 17, 18, 24, 25, 29, 32,
  52, 53, 59, 71, 78, 86, 140, 142,
  150, 153, 163, 168, 175, 176
Carpet, Turkish, 56
Cassatt, Mary, 175
Chairs, 17, 35, 37, 100, 110, 115, 189,
  190, 195, 196, 197, 199
  "Adirondack chair," 164; armchair,
  17 (German), 32, 35, 37, 42, 43, 48,
  49, 52, 53, 68, 92, 102, 108, 111,
  112 (Empire style), 122, 140, 149,
  156, 172, 173, 185, 193, 206
  (Graves), 207; Baltimore, 104;
  bannister-back, 37, 48, 82;
  Barcelona, 187; bench, 56, 72, 84,
  140; bow-back, 49; Breuer, 179,

206; campaign, 104; Chippendale,
37, 40, 50, 75; corner, 41, 44;
courting, 176; curule, 92, 95, 98;
dining, 118, 153, 189, 197; easy, 42,
52, 179; fan-back, 68; Federal, 76;
gentlemen's, 192; gondola, 101;
Gothic Revival, 118; Hitchcock, 104,
111; horn, 157; ice-cream-parlor, 18;
klismos, 92, 98, 110; ladder-back,
49; lolling, 26, 61, 63, 78, 98, 164;
lounge, 199, 205, 206; love seat, 20,
200; Martha Washington, 47, 61;
Mission style, 175; Morris, 151, 155;
painted, 76, 107; plank, 17; planter's
26, 62, 78; rockers, 121, 129, 134,
140, 141, 142, 176, 181, 182, 183;
saber-legged, 181; settle, 39, 49; side,
29, 37, 40, 41, 44, 50, 52, 53, 63,
75, 95, 105, 108, 118, 142, 144
(Gothic Revival), 155, 175, 181, 185,
203; slat-back, 82, 111, 135, 140,
142; slipper, 120; thumb-back, 20;
Wassily, 206; Windsor, 48, 49, 53,
55, 68, 71, 106, 108, 130; wing,
181, 183; writing, 68
Chandeliers—see lighting
Chests, 37, 42, 51, 98, 107, 119, 132
  blanket (German), 17;
  camphorwood, 67, 68, 72; cellarette,
  81; on-chest, 42, 47; cabinet-style,
  141; of drawers, 37, 42, 43, 51, 141;
  desk on, 125; child's, 7;
  Chippendale reproduction, 5;
  dresser-style, 49, 126, 139, 143
  (Gothic Revival); Hadley, 33; linen,
  75; pine, 20; six-board, 44; storage,
  86; toy, 183; triple, 31; trunk, 74
Chippendale style, 17, 35
Chippendale, Thomas, 17, 18, 37, 40,
  47, 50, 55, 56, 75, 203
Clocks, 33, 53, 77, 88 (banjo), 122,
  153, 166, 170, 176
Colonial style, 31, 44
Colonial Revival style, 119
Cupboards, 25, 32, 35, 40, 43, 44, 48,
  50, 52, 55, 56, 71, 74, 81, 84, 105,
  108, 133, 135, 141, 153, 181

Damask, wool, 35
Decoys, 21, 67, 68, 71, 105, 138, 161,
  162, 176

Desks, 40, 42, 48, 52, 53, 63, 68, 74,
  75, 79, 91, 96, 100, 108, 123, 124,
  125, 157, 159, 170, 181, 196
Deskey, Donald, 190, 191

Eames, Charles, 197, 199, 206
Eastlake, 118, 119
Egyptian Revival style, 118, 119
Elfe, Thomas, 40, 41, 108
Elizabethan Revival style, 117, 118, 119,
  121, 126
Empire style, 95, 98, 104,
  112 (armchair)

Fabric, French design, 207
Federal style, 82, 87, 88
Fireboard, Boston, 68
Fireplace equipment, 68, 111, 144, 174
Fireplaces, 122, 153, 183, 202
Flasks, glass, 87
Floorclothes, 111
Floors, 20, 21, 26, 43, 94,
  110, 206 (rubber), 207
Frankl, Paul Theodore, 182, 193
French Empire style, 98

Georgian style
  Gunston Hall, 29; house, 29, 31;
  plantation, 29
Glass, 55, 81, 87, 132, 139, 143
  (candlestick), 143 (pitcher), 158, 173,
  193
Glassware, 52, 88 (tumblers), 166
Gothic Revival style, 118, 119, 121, 143
Graves, Michael, 205, 206
Greek Revival style, 91, 95, 101, 102,
  118, 120
Gropius, Walter, 182

Hall, John, 118
Hepplewhite, 59, 61, 64, 68 (style), 76, 82, 87
Hacienda, 17
High-tech, 185, 207
Hitchcock, Lambert, 97, 99, 104, 106, 107, 108, 110, 111, 112
Hoffman, Josef, 182
Houdon, Jean Antoine, 92
Houses, 32, 35, 48, 66, 81, 100, 104, 108, 121, 139, 172, 181, 203, 205
   Arlington, 78, 120; barn, 202; Bartow-Pell, 102; beach, 127; Casa San Ysidro, 84, 86; cedar-shingled, 66, 202; Charleston, 19th century, 26; Colonial, 116; cottage, 44, 67, 104, 105, 106; Craft House, 5, 56; Edgewater, 91, 92, 94, 95, 96; farmhouse, 44, 98, 136; Federal, 80, 82, 116; Gramercy, 193; Georgian-style, 29; "glass," 187; Greek Revival style, 78, 101, 112, 116, 118, 120; Gunston Hall, 29, 31, 47; Hanger, 121; Highland, 7, 8, 179, 183; hunting lodge, 162; Lake Erie Hall, 61; log, 132, 133, 134; Log Folly, 40, 41, 42, 43; Lookout Mountain, 18, 132, 133; Manigault, 63; Melrose, 116, 118, 124; Monroe Savings Bank, 108; Nantucket, 19th century, 24; New England frame, 32; Old Merchant's House, 101,

120; Post-Modern, 205; Radio City Music Hall, 190; Nathaniel Russell, 59, 61, 87; salt box, 32, 34, 37; Taliesin III, 147; townhouse, 80, 85, 99, 101, 128; Victorian, 114; Winedale, 119; Frank Lloyd Wright, 147
Hubbard, Elbert, 156
Huntboard, 16, 59, 64
Hunter, Dard, 155

International style, 182

Jackson, Robert, 94
Japanese Revival, 119
Johnson, Philip, 187

Kurz and Allison, 174, 195

Lafayette, Marquis de, 96
Lampshades, 66, 144, 175 (silk), 206—see also lighting
Lannuier, Charles Honore, 94, 96, 98
Le Corbusier, 202
Lighting and Lamps
   Argand gas, 101; Art Deco, 188; Astral, 101; brass, 80, 127, 135, 143 (gaslight); brass bases for, 175; chandelier, 24, 56, 116, 175 (brass), 206 (etched glass); desk, 207; factory, 202; floor, 189; Galle, 173; Lalique, 173; sconces, 52, 56, 110, 111, 143; stoneware, 67; student, 174; table, 153, 170, 188, 191, 206 (Art Deco); Tiffany, 151, 153, 175; torchere, 193; "up light," 207; wall brackets for, 94; wisteria, 172; Wright, Frank Lloyd, 146
Livingston, Robert, 91
Louis XVI style, 61, 119

Mantelpieces, 42, 68, 82, 86, 101, 143, 161, 174, 181
Marcotte, Leon, 119
Mason, George, 29, 31, 47
Medieval style, 34
Meier, Richard, 204
Metalwork, 50, 51, 55, 56, 71, 79, 84, 86, 87, 110, 125, 167

Ming dynasty, 43
Mirrors, 18, 43, 80, 94, 95, 96, 99, 102, 104, 116, 137, 139, 193
Mission style, 27, 149, 156, 166, 175
Moore, Abel Buel, 92
Moorish style, 123
Morris, William, 156, 176
Mortise and tenon, 32, 55

Navajo Indians, 182
Nelson, George, 200
Neoclassical style, 91, 111, 120, 131
Noguchi, Isamu, 196
Nylander, Jane, 87
Nylander, Richard C., 87

Oriental style, 123

Paintings and portraits, 24, 29, 43, 44, 47, 48, 49, 55, 56, 64, 68, 71, 80, 92, 94, 104, 105, 107, 112, 132, 135, 137, 140, 156, 161, 202—see also art, posters and prints
   Brooke, Richard N., 49; bultos, 84; Eichholtz, 92; folk, 53; Holmes, David Bryan, 71; Lang, Louis, 102; miniatures, 80; Muhl, Roger, 20; Phillips, Ammi, 29; Remington, Frederick, 157; reproduction, 56; retablos, 84; silhouette, 144; Stuart, Gilbert, 91; watercolors, 80, 111, 112; Warhol, Andy, 206
Palladian style, 26, 30, 31
Phyfe, Duncan, 76, 77, 91, 92, 94, 95, 98, 110
Picasso, Pablo, 182
Pie safe, 112, 135
Pilgrim Century style, 32, 33
Pillar-and-scroll furniture, 104
Porcelain and pottery, 77, 84, 110, 152, 156
   Brittany ware, 24; candlesticks, 71; Canton, 71; Chinese Export ware, 29, 59, 61, 64, 87, 105; crafts, 30, 165; Delftware, 37; houses, 138; humidor, 175; hunting dogs, 161; Lenox, 176; majolica, 24; Meissen, 64; polychrome, 40, 48, 86; Pueblo, 86; redware, 43; salt-glaze ware, 40; service, 87; spatter ware, 24;

Staffordshire, 181, 183; stoneware, 66, 105, 143 (salt-glazed); teapot, 50; urns, 110; Zuni, 86
Posters and prints, 82, 183—see also art, paintings and portraits
   Art Deco, 206; Audubon, 181; battle, 174; chromoliths, 174; George Washington, 87; "La Toilette," 175; Sarg, 195; war, 174; Warhol, 206
Post-Modern style, 205, 207
Pugin, A.W.N., 119

Queen Anne style, 29, 34, 35, 37, 55, 99, 121
Quervelle, Anthony, 98
   chest, 119
Quilts and coverlets, 20, 26, 42, 51, 72, 106, 126, 127, 138, 165, 170, 175, 181, 183, 202—see also blankets

Regency style, 98
Renaissance Revival style, 119, 122, 125, 151
Renwick, William R., 159
Revere, Paul, 35
Rococo Revival style, 114, 116, 119, 120, 122, 125, 128
Roof, gambrel, 34
Rohde, Gilbert, 188, 196
Rooms
   attic, 127; bar, 53; bath, 176; bed, 20, 22, 42, 47, 51, 63, 72, 96, 97, 98, 106, 119, 120, 126, 129, 138, 156, 158, 171, 183; breakfast, 43, 49; chapel, 84; dining, 24, 37, 64, 71, 76, 78, 84, 99, 110, 112, 118, 147, 153, 166, 179, 181, 185, 189, 191; drawing, 61, 95, 102, 116; entrance hall, 21, 26, 55, 80, 94, 124; family, 26, 82; front hall, 48, 102; gallery, 181; hallway, 8, 43, 136, 137;

kitchen, 8, 18, 23, 37, 105, 135, 168, 169, 183; library, 40, 41, 48, 67, 68, 82, 86, 92, 102, 150, 157, 165, 195; living, 52, 66, 82, 99, 136, 140, 141, 149, 153, 167, 181, 187, 188, 191, 202; loft/office, 174; parlor, 31 (formal), 33, 35, 56, 63 (formal Federal), 100, 101, 120, 121; recreation, 172, 173; showroom, 205; sitting room, 91, 139

Roycroft, 152, 153, 155, 156, 157

Rugs, 22, 23, 44, 92, 134, 137
    bed, 47; "faithpur" dhurrie, 4; hooked, 7, 22, 23, 67, 72, 126, 133, 161, 176; India, 167; *jerga*, 84, 86; Navajo, 17, 86; needlepoint, 175; Oriental, 181; rag, 143; reproduction, 116; Savonnerie, 102; Suzanne and Cleland Selby, 176; Transylvanian prayer, 56; William Thompson, 92; wool, 118; George Wells, 22, 23

Ruskin, John, 156

Saarinen, Eero, 182, 185, 197, 199, 206

Saarinen, Eliel, 182, 189

Scrank, German, 17

Seating systems, 200, 207

Secretary, 63, 79 (butler's), 142

Seignoret, Francois, 100, 101

Settee, 16 (high-backed), 144, 163, 181, 183

Shaker furniture, 140, 141, 142, 144, 145

Sheraton, Thomas, 61, 68, 77, 98, 108 (style, English)

Ship model, 105

Sideboards, 16, 59, 64, 68, 76, 88, 118, 125, 151, 203

Silver,
    beaker, 56; sauce dish, 79; service, 50; teapot, 51; tongs, 55

Silversmiths, 35, 51

Sofas, 26, 35, 41, 44, 62, 63 (cabriole), 82, 92, 95, 99, 100, 102, 120, 140, 144, 163, 176, 181, 182, 187, 193, 200

Stands
    sewing, 141; Shaker, 142; smoking, 155

Stencil, 8 (Pennsylvania style), 111 (pineapple)

Stencilling, 111, 137

Stickley, Gustav, 149, 150, 151, 156, 166, 170, 175

Stools, 20, 23, 47, 155, 199

Stoves, 8, 168

Stuart, Gilbert, 91

Tables, 33, 37, 53, 63, 71, 75, 80, 92, 105, 108, 110, 121, 135, 137, 189, 190, 193, 196
    Barcelona, 187, 206; buffet, 189; card, 82, 94, 102; drum, 99, 102, 114; chopping, 134; conference/dining, 204; console, 136, 155; cricket, 67; cricket bedside, 72; dining, 50, 71, 77, 84, 118, 153, 189, 193, 203, 204; dressing, 29, 47, 96, 106; drop-leaf, 50, 68, 77; folding, 37; fruitwood, 71; gaming, 41, 98; gate-leg, 32, 33, 37, 44, 48, 49; "Grand Rapids" style, 8; Kioto, 205; lady's worktable, 97; library, 149, 153; Louis XVI style, 17; lyre-based, 94; marble-topped, 23, 43, 114; pedestal, 8, 52, 155, 167, 185; Pembroke, 41, 63 (tea), 87; pier, 92, 94, 95, 102; sausage-grinding, 136; sawbuck, 17; serving, 18; Sheraton, 76, 77; slab, 41; stretcher-based, 48; taboret, 155; tavern, 37, 53; tea, 24, 35, 51, 52, 62, 99; tilt-top, 51, 68, 78, 99; toilet, 97; turtle-top, 116; two-tier, 26; worktable, 80, 92, 97

Tableware, 24, 29, 49, 50, 59, 71, 76, 96, 98, 99, 105, 143, 152, 167, 193

Terry, Eli, 108

Thomas, Seth, 108

Thompson, William, 92

Thonet, Michael, 193

Tiffany, Louis Comfort, 151, 156, 172, 175

Tools, 137, 168, 182

Toolshed, 131

Town, A. Hayes, 130, 131

Toys
    checkerboard, 176; collection, 138; lead soldiers, 174; metal, 133; rocking horse, 72; swing, 128, 176; wooden, 133

Tumblers, three-mold, 88

Twig furniture, 162, 163, 176

Utensils
    boot scraper, 131; food chopper, 169; rug beaters, 169; sugar tongs, 55

Van der Rohe, Ludwig Mies, 182, 187, 206

Vases, 94, 152, 155, 157

Victorian style, 26, 31, 44, 74, 114, 120, 122, 124, 125, 127, 129, 137, 138, 139, 143, 144, 170, 171

Vignelli, Massimo and Lella, 205

Wallcoverings, 26, 55, 88, 111, 112, 121, 127, 129, 137, 143 (French), 144, 170, 202, 206 (Art Greco), 207—*see also walls*

Walls, 21, 23, 24, 26, 31, 33, 39, 40, 47, 82, 86, 95, 102, 108, 111, 183—*see also wallcoverings*

Wardrobe, 16, 96, 98

Washstand, 96, 98, 106

Weather vanes, 44, 53, 143, 144

Werkstatte, Vienna, 182

White, Stanford, 151

Wicker, 20, 129, 139, 158, 164, 195

William and Mary style, 32, 34, 35, 37, 48

Windows, 26, 27, 44, 72, 158, 175

Window treatments, 23, 42, 55, 88, 102, 106, 112 (swag and jabot), 116, 143 (Victorian), 144

Wood, David, 53

Woolsey, David, 172

Wright, Frank Lloyd, 146, 147, 151, 179, 204
    fabric design, 207

This patriotic copper weather vane is another charming piece in Steve Miller's American Folk Art collection [R.G. #40].

DECORATING WITH AMERICANA

Designed by
Michael Shroyer, New York

Text composed in Bembo by
Fine Composition, New York, New York

Color separation by
Capitol Engraving Company,
Nashville, Tennessee

Printing and binding by
Kingsport Press, Inc.
Kingsport, Tennessee

Endleaves are
Linen weave, Early American
Colonial white

Cover cloth is
Holliston sail cloth black #16075